Important Instruction

Students, Parents, and Teachers can use the URL or QR code provided below to access two full-length Lumos GMAS practice tests. Please note that these assessments are provided in the Online format only.

URL	QR Code
Visit the URL below and place the book access code **http://www.lumoslearning.com/a/tedbooks** **Access Code: GMASMG5-27348-S**	(QR code)

Lumos Learning
Developed by Expert Teachers

GMAS Online Assessments and 5th Grade Math Practice Workbook, Student Copy

Contributing Author   -   **April LoTempio**
Executive Producer   -   **Mukunda Krishnaswamy**
Designer and Illustrator -   **Sowmya R.**

First Edition - 2020

NGA Center/CCSSO are the sole owners and developers of the Common Core State Standards, which does not sponsor or endorse this product. © Copyright 2010. National Governors Association Center for Best Practices and Council of Chief State School Officers.

Georgia Department of Education is not affiliated to Lumos Learning. Georgia Department of Education, was not involved in the production of, and does not endorse these products or this site.

ISBN-10: 1542666600

ISBN-13: 978-1542666602

Printed in the United States of America

For permissions and additional information contact us

Lumos Information Services, LLC
PO Box 1575, Piscataway, NJ 08855-1575
http://www.LumosLearning.com

Email: support@lumoslearning.com
Tel: (732) 384-0146
Fax: (866) 283-6471

Developed by Expert Teachers

INTRODUCTION

About Lumos tedBook for GMAS Test Practice:

This book is specifically designed to improve student achievement on the GMAS. Students perform at their best on standardized tests when they feel comfortable with the test content as well as the test format. Lumos tedBook for GMAS test ensures this with meticulously designed practice that adheres to the guidelines provided by the GMAS for the number of questions, standards, difficulty level, sessions, question types, and duration.

About Lumos Smart Test Prep:

With more than a decade of experience and expertise in developing practice resources for standardized tests, Lumos Learning has developed the most efficient methodology to help students succeed on the state assessments (See Figure 1).

Lumos Smart Test Prep Methodology offers students realistic GMAS assessment rehearsal along with providing an efficient pathway to overcome each proficiency gap.

The process starts with students taking the online diagnostic assessment. This online diagnostic test will help assess students' proficiency levels in various standards. With the completion of this diagnostic assessment, Lumos generates a personalized study plan with a standard checklist based on student performance in the online diagnostic test. Parents and educators can use this study plan to remediate the proficiency gaps with targeted standards-based practice available in the workbook.

After student completes the targeted remedial practice, they should attempt the second online GMAS practice test. Upon finishing the second assessment, Lumos will generate another individualized study plan by identifying topics that require more practice. Based on these practice suggestions, further skill building activities can be planned to help students gain comprehensive mastery needed to ensure success on the state assessment.

Lumos Smart Test Prep Methodology

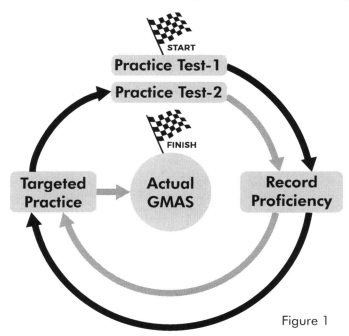

Figure 1

Table of Contents

Sign Up Online

GMAS

Grade 5 Math Practice

Unlock Digital Access

2 GMAS Practice Tests

3 Math Domains

Sign Up Now

Url: https://LumosLearning/a/tedbooks

Access Code: GMASMG5-27348-S

Access GMAS Test Practice Resources On Your Mobile Device

Online Access

for

GMAS Practice

Printed Workbook

for

Skills Practice

Download Lumos StepUp App
from Google Play Store or Apple App Store

After installing the StepUp App, scan this **QR Code** via **tedBook** section of the mobile app

Chapter 1

Lumos Smart Test Prep Methodology

Step 1: Access Online GMAS Practice Test

The online GMAS practice tests mirror the actual Georgia Milestones Assessment System (GMAS) in the number of questions, item types, test duration, test tools, and more.

After completing the test, your student will receive immediate feedback with detailed reports on standards mastery and a personalized study plan to overcome any learning gaps. With this study plan, use the next section of the workbook to practice.

Use the URL and access code provided below or scan the QR code to access the first GMAS practice test to get started.

URL	QR Code
Visit the URL below and place the book access code **http://www.lumoslearning.com/a/tedbooks** **Access Code: GMASMG5-27348-S**	

Step 2: Review the Personalized Study Plan Online

After students complete the online Practice Test 1, they can access their individualized study plan from the table of contents (Figure 2) Parents and Teachers can also review the study plan through their Lumos account (parent or teacher) portal.

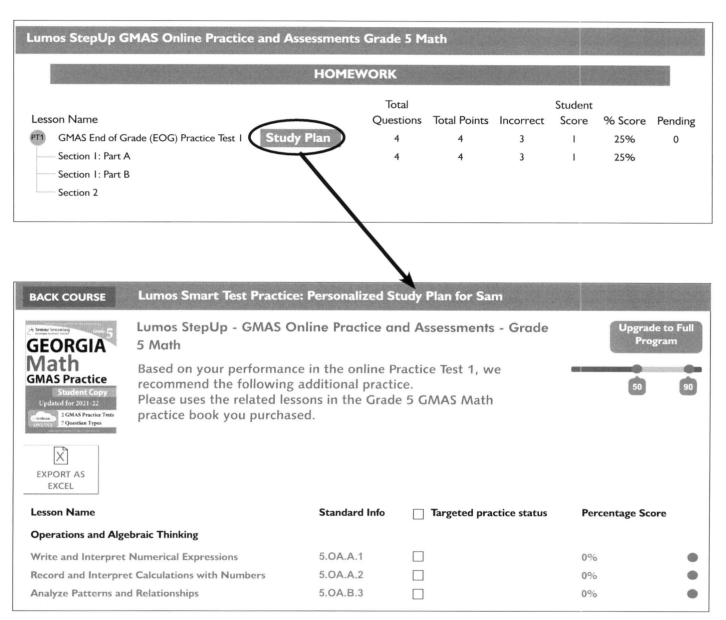

Figure 2

Step 3: Complete Targeted Practice

Using the information provided in the study plan report, complete the targeted practice using the appropriate lessons to overcome proficiency gaps. With lesson names included in the study plan, find the appropriate topics in this workbook and answer the questions provided. Marking the completed lessons in the study plan after each practice session is recommended. (See Figure 3)

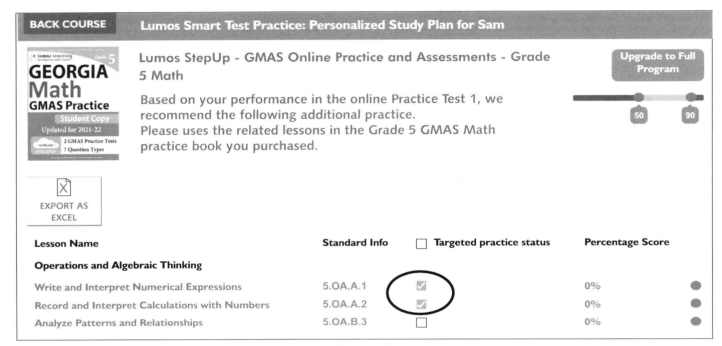

Figure 3

Step 4: Access the Practice Test 2 Online

After completing the targeted practice in this workbook, students should attempt the second GMAS practice test online. Using the student login name and password, login to the Lumos website to complete the second practice test.

Step 5: Repeat Targeted Practice

Repeat the targeted practice as per Step 3 using the second study plan report for Practice test 2 after completion of the second GMAS rehearsal.

Visit http://www.lumoslearning.com/a/lstp for more information on Lumos Smart Test Prep Methodology or Scan the QR Code

Test Taking Tips

1) **The day before the test,** make sure you get a good night's sleep.

2) **On the day of the test,** be sure to eat a good hearty breakfast! Also, be sure to arrive at school on time.

3) **During the test:**

- **Read each question carefully.**

  - Do not spend too much time on any one question. Work steadily through all questions in the section.
  - Attempt all the questions even if you are not sure of some answers.
  - If you run into a difficult question, eliminate as many choices as you can and then pick the best one from the remaining choices. Intelligent guessing will help you increase your score.
  - Also, mark the question so that if you have extra time, you can return to it after you reach the end of the section.
  - Some questions may refer to a graph, chart, or other kind of picture. Carefully review the infographics before answering the question.
  - Be sure to include explanations for your written responses and show all work.

- **While Answering Multiple-choice (EBSR) questions.**

  - Select the bubble corresponding to your answer choice.
  - Read all of the answer choices, even if think you have found the correct answer.

- **While Answering TECR questions.**

  - Read the directions of each question. Some might ask you to drag something, others to select, and still others to highlight. Follow all instructions of the question (or questions if it is in multiple parts)

Chapter 2:
Operations and Algebraic Thinking

Lesson 1: Write and Interpret Numerical Expressions & Patterns

You can scan the QR code given below or use the url to access additional EdSearch resources including videos and mobile apps related to *Write and Interpret Numerical Expressions*.

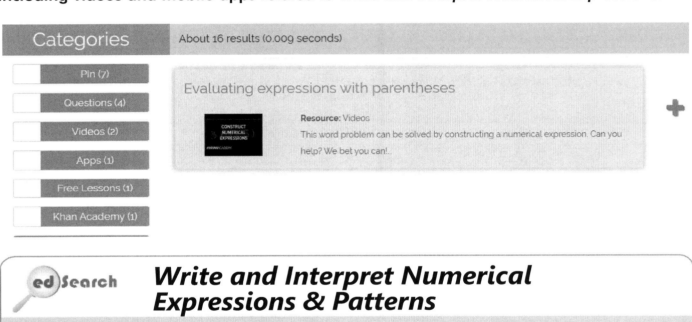

Categories

About 16 results (0.009 seconds)

Pin (7)

Questions (4)

Videos (2)

Apps (1)

Free Lessons (1)

Khan Academy (1)

Evaluating expressions with parentheses

Resource: Videos

This word problem can be solved by constructing a numerical expression. Can you help? We bet you can!..

ed Search   *Write and Interpret Numerical Expressions & Patterns*

URL	QR Code
http://www.lumoslearning.com/a/5oaa1	

1. Which of the following number sentences models the Associative Property of Multiplication? Circle the correct answer choice.

   Ⓐ 80 x 5 = (40 x 5) + (40 x 5)
   Ⓑ (11 x 6) x 7 = 11 x (6 x 7)
   Ⓒ 3 x 4 x 2 = 2 x 4 x 3
   Ⓓ 44 x 1 = 44

2. What is the value of 2 x [5-(6 ÷3)]?

3. Identify the expression that equals 2?

   Ⓐ [(3 x 2) + 4] ÷ 5
   Ⓑ 2 x [(5 x 4) ÷ 10]
   Ⓒ 12 - [(4 + 8) ÷ 3]

4. Rewrite the equation below substituting a number value for 'a' and an operation for the question mark that would result in a solution of 10.
   20 ÷ [5 - (a ? 9)] = 10

5. **Evaluate the expression (8 x 6) + (8-3)?**

Ⓐ 53
Ⓑ 48
Ⓒ 64
Ⓓ 81

6. **Where must the parentheses be in the following expression so that the answer is 6?**
    20 - 8 ÷ 2

Ⓐ 20 - (8 ÷ 2)
Ⓑ (20 - 8) ÷ 2

7. **Evaluate the expression 4 x (2 + 1) + 6.**

Ⓐ 18
Ⓑ 15
Ⓒ 21
Ⓓ 16

8. **In a drawing class, crayons were distributed to 12 students. Six of the students got packets that had 8 crayons and the other six got packets that had 10 crayons. How many crayons were distributed in all?**

Ⓐ 110
Ⓑ 108
Ⓒ 100
Ⓓ 112

9. **Jeremy had 20 books which he arranged in 4 shelves of a rack. His brother, Brandon takes away 4 books from each of the shelves. How many books are there now in each shelf?**

Ⓐ 4
Ⓑ 5
Ⓒ 8
Ⓓ 1

10. **Mary has 15 chocolates that she wants to put into packs of 3. She wants to give these packs to 4 of her friends. Choose the expression that fits the story.**

Ⓐ (15 ÷ 3) + 4
Ⓑ (15 × 3) + 4
Ⓒ (15 × 3) − 4
Ⓓ (15 ÷ 3) − 4

Chapter 2

Lesson 2: Record and Interpret Calculations with Numbers

You can scan the QR code given below or use the url to access additional EdSearch resources including videos and mobile apps related to *Record and Interpret Calculations with Numbers.*

 **Record and Interpret Calculations with Numbers**

URL	QR Code
http://www.lumoslearning.com/a/5oaa2	

1. **Which expression shows 10 more than the quotient of 72 divided by 8?**

    Ⓐ (10 + 72) ÷ 8
    Ⓑ (72 ÷ 8) + 10
    Ⓒ 72 ÷ (8 + 10)
    Ⓓ 8 ÷ (72 + 10)

2. **Which expression shows 75 minus the product of 12 and 4?**

    Ⓐ (75 – 12) x 4
    Ⓑ (12 x 4) – 75
    Ⓒ 75 – (12 + 4)
    Ⓓ 75 – (12 x 4)

3. **Jamie purchased 10 cases of soda for a party. Each case holds 24 cans. He also purchased 3 packs of juice. Each pack of juice has 6 cans. Which expression represents the number of cans he purchased?**

    Ⓐ (10 x 24) + (3 x 6)
    Ⓑ (10 + 24) x (3 + 6)
    Ⓒ 10 x (24 + 6)
    Ⓓ 10 x 24 x 3 x 6

4. **Olivia had 42 pieces of candy. She kept 9 pieces for herself and then divided the rest evenly among her three friends. Which expression best represents the number of candy each friend received?**

    Ⓐ (42 ÷ 3) - 9
    Ⓑ (42 – 9) ÷ 3
    Ⓒ 42 ÷ (9 – 3)
    Ⓓ 42 – (9 ÷ 3)

5. **Which is true about the solution to 8 x (467 + 509)?**

    Ⓐ It is a number in the ten thousands.
    Ⓑ It is an odd number.
    Ⓒ It is eight times greater than the sum of 467 and 509.
    Ⓓ It is 509 more than the product of 8 and 467.

6. **Which is true about the solution to (3,259 – 741) ÷ 3?**

   Ⓐ It is one third as much as the difference between 3,259 and 741.
   Ⓑ It is 741 less than the quotient of 3,259 divided by 3.
   Ⓒ It is a whole number.
   Ⓓ It is a number in the thousands.

7. **Part A**
   Which of these expressions would result in the greatest number?

   Ⓐ 420 – (28 x 13)
   Ⓑ 420 + 28 + 13
   Ⓒ (420 – 28) x 13
   Ⓓ 420 + (28 x 13)

   Part B
   Which of these expressions would result in the smallest number?

   Ⓐ 684 – (47 + 6)
   Ⓑ 684 – 47 – 6
   Ⓒ (684 – 47) x 6
   Ⓓ 684 – (47 x 6)

8. **Each of the 25 students in a class sold 7 items for a fundraiser. Their teacher also sold 13 items. Which expression best represents the number of items they sold in all? Circle the correct answer choice**

   Ⓐ 25 x (7 + 13)
   Ⓑ 13 + (25 x 7)
   Ⓒ 7 x (25 + 13)
   Ⓓ 25 + 7 + 13

9. **Mario had $75. He doubled that amount by mowing his neighbor's lawn all summer. Then he spent $47 on new sneakers. Which expression best represents the amount of money he now has?**

   Ⓐ (75 x 2) - 47
   Ⓑ (75 + 75) ÷ 47
   Ⓒ 47 – (75 + 2)
   Ⓓ 75 + 2 - 47

Chapter 2

Lesson 3: Analyze Patterns and Relationships

You can scan the QR code given below or use the url to access additional EdSearch resources including videos and mobile apps related to *Analyze Patterns and Relationships*.

 **Analyze Patterns and Relationships**

URL	QR Code
http://www.lumoslearning.com/a/5oab3	

1. **Which set of numbers completes the function table?**
    Rule: multiply by 3

Input	Output
1	☐
2	☐
5	15
8	☐
12	☐

   Ⓐ 4, 5, 11, 15
   Ⓑ 3, 6, 24, 36
   Ⓒ 3, 6, 32, 48
   Ⓓ 11, 12, 18, 112

2. **Which set of numbers completes the function table?**
    Rule: add 4, then divide by 2

Input	Output
4	☐
6	☐
10	7
22	☐
40	☐

   Ⓐ 1, 3, 19, 37
   Ⓑ 10, 12, 28, 46
   Ⓒ 4, 5, 13, 22
   Ⓓ 16, 20, 52, 88

3. **Which set of coordinate pairs matches the function table?**
   Rule: multiply by 2, then subtract 1

Input	Output
5	☐
9	17
14	☐
25	☐

   Ⓐ (5 , 9), (9 , 17), (14 , 27), (25 , 49)
   Ⓑ (5 , 9), (14 , 25), (9 , 17), (27 , 49)
   Ⓒ (5 , 9), (9 , 17), (17 , 14), (14 , 25)
   Ⓓ (5 , 11), (9 , 17), (14 , 29), (25 , 51)

4. **Which set of coordinate pairs matches the function table?**
   Rule: divide by 3, then add 2

Input	Output
9	☐
15	7
27	☐
33	☐

   Ⓐ (9 , 1), (15 , 7), (27 , 19), (33 , 25)
   Ⓑ (9 , 5), (15 , 7), (27 , 11), (33 , 13)
   Ⓒ (9 , 11), (15 , 7), (27 , 29), (33 , 35)
   Ⓓ (9 , 15), (15 , 7), (7 , 27), (27 , 33)

5. **Which set of numbers completes the function table?**
    Rule: subtract 4

Input	Output
☐	1
7	3
☐	7
☐	10
☐	15

Ⓐ 0, 3, 6, 11
Ⓑ 3, 10, 17, 25
Ⓒ 4, 28, 40, 60
Ⓓ 5, 11, 14, 19

6. **Which set of numbers completes the function table?**
    Rule: add 1, then multiply by 5

Input	Output
☐	5
2	15
☐	20
☐	35
☐	55

Ⓐ 2, 5, 15, 20
Ⓑ 1, 4, 7, 11
Ⓒ 30, 105, 180, 280
Ⓓ 0, 3, 6, 10

7. **Which rule describes the function table?**

x	y
11	5
14	8
21	15
28	22

Ⓐ Add 3
Ⓑ Subtract 6
Ⓒ Subtract 1, then divide by 2
Ⓓ Divide by 2, Add 1

8. **Which rule describes the function table?**

x	y
4	4
7	10
13	22
20	36

Ⓐ Multiply by 2, then subtract 4
Ⓑ Add zero
Ⓒ Add 3
Ⓓ Subtract 1, then multiply by 2

9. **Which describes the graph of this function plotted on a coordinate grid?**

x	y
11	5
14	8
21	15
28	22

Ⓐ A curving line
Ⓑ A horizontal line
Ⓒ An upward sloping line
Ⓓ A downward sloping line

10. **Which type of function would result in a graph that looks like this?**

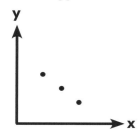

Ⓐ One in which x and y increase at fixed rates
Ⓑ One in which x and y decrease at fixed rates
Ⓒ One in which x decreases while y increases
Ⓓ One in which x increases while y decreases

11. **Consider the following two number sequences:**
    x: begin at 2, add 3
    y: begin at 4, add 6
    Which describes the relationship between the number sequences?

Ⓐ The terms in sequence y are two more than the terms in sequence x.
Ⓑ The terms in sequence y are six times the terms in sequence x.
Ⓒ The terms in sequence y are two times the terms in sequence x.
Ⓓ The terms in sequence y are half as much as the terms in sequence x.

12. **Consider the following two number sequences:**
    x: begin at 1, multiply by 2
    y: begin at 2, multiply by 2
    Which describes the relationship between the number sequences?

    Ⓐ The terms in sequence y are one more than the terms in sequence x.
    Ⓑ The terms in sequence y are two times the terms in sequence x.
    Ⓒ The terms in sequence y are two more than the terms in sequence x.
    Ⓓ The terms in sequence y are half as much as the terms in sequence x.

13. **Consider the following number sequence:**
    x: begin at 5, add 6
    Which would result in a relationship in which y is always three more than x?

    Ⓐ y: begin at 8, add 6
    Ⓑ y: begin at 5, add 9
    Ⓒ y: begin at 8, add 9
    Ⓓ y: begin at 2, add 6

14. **Consider the following number sequence:**
    x: begin at 4, multiply by 2
    Which would result in a relationship in which y is always half as much as x?

    Ⓐ y: begin at 4, multiply by 4
    Ⓑ y: begin at 4, multiply by ½
    Ⓒ y: begin at 2, multiply by 1
    Ⓓ y: begin at 2, multiply by 2

15. Use the table to answer the following question.
     What value of x would result in a y value of 16?

x	y
0	-2
3	7
4	10
9	25
12	34
10	38
5	13
	16

Ⓐ x = 6
Ⓑ x = 7
Ⓒ x = 8
Ⓓ x = 11

16. Consider the following pattern:
     7, 9, 4, 6, 1, . . .
     If the pattern continued, what would be the first negative number to appear?
     Write your answer in the box given below.

_____

17. What is the next number in this pattern? Fill in the blank with the next number of the pattern.

     168, 152, 136, 120, _____

18. Kevin has been cutting lawns to earn some extra spending money. The first week he worked, he earned $10.00. Each successive week, for the next three weeks, he earned twice what he had earned the week before. How much money, in all, did he earn during the first four weeks of work? Write your answer along with the steps by which you arrived at the answer in the box given below.

19. To find the next number in this pattern, multiply the term by 3 and then add 1.
The first three terms in the pattern are 1, 4, and 13.
What would the fifth term be? Circle the correct answer choice

Ⓐ 121
Ⓑ 120
Ⓒ 129
Ⓓ 111

End of Operations and Algebraic Thinking

LumosLearning.com

Chapter 3:
Number & Operations in Base Ten

Lesson 1: Place Value

You can scan the QR code given below or use the url to access additional EdSearch resources including videos and mobile apps related to *Place Value*.

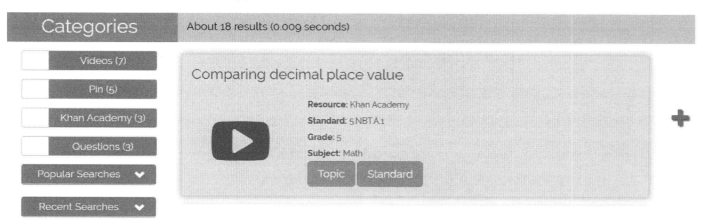

Categories   About 18 results (0.009 seconds)

Videos (7)
Pin (5)
Khan Academy (3)
Questions (3)
Popular Searches ⌄
Recent Searches ⌄

Comparing decimal place value

Resource: Khan Academy
Standard: 5.NBT.A.1
Grade: 5
Subject: Math

Topic   Standard

---

ed)Search   *Place Value*

URL	QR Code
http://www.lumoslearning.com/a/5nbta1	

1. In the number 913,874 which digit is in the ten thousands place?

    Ⓐ 8
    Ⓑ 1
    Ⓒ 9
    Ⓓ 3

2. In the number 7.2065 which digit is in the thousandths place?

    Ⓐ 5
    Ⓑ 2
    Ⓒ 0
    Ⓓ 6

3. Which number is equivalent to 8/10?

    Ⓐ 0.8
    Ⓑ 8.0
    Ⓒ 0.08
    Ⓓ 0.008

4. What is the equivalent of 4 and 3/100?

    Ⓐ 40.3
    Ⓑ 0.403
    Ⓒ 4.03
    Ⓓ 403.0

5. In the number 16,428,095 what is the value of the digit 6?

    Ⓐ 6 million
    Ⓑ 60 thousand
    Ⓒ 60 million
    Ⓓ 600 thousand

6. What is the value of 9 in the number 5,802.109

    Ⓐ 9 thousand
    Ⓑ 9 tenths
    Ⓒ 9 thousandths
    Ⓓ 9 hundredths

7. **Which comparison is correct?**

Ⓐ 50.5 = 50.05
Ⓑ 0.05 = 0.50
Ⓒ 0.005 = 500.0
Ⓓ 0.50 = 0.500

8. **Which number is one hundredth less than 406.51?**

Ⓐ 406.41
Ⓑ 406.50
Ⓒ 306.51
Ⓓ 406.01

9. **Which of the following numbers is greater than 8.4?**

Ⓐ 8.41
Ⓑ 8.40
Ⓒ 8.14
Ⓓ 8.04

10. **Which of the following numbers is less than 2.17?**

Ⓐ 21.7
Ⓑ 2.71
Ⓒ 2.170
Ⓓ 2.07

11. **When comparing 385.24 with 452.38 which of the following statements are correct? Select all that apply.**

Ⓐ The digit 3 in 385.24 is 1000 times greater than the 3 in 452.38.
Ⓑ The digit 5 is ten times less in 452.38 than in 385.24.
Ⓒ The digit 8 is 100 times more in 385.24 than in 452.38.
Ⓓ The digit 2 is 10 times more in 452.38 than in 385.24

12. Read each statement and indicate whether it is true or false.

	True	False
The 5 in 570.22 is ten times greater than 5 in 456.1	◯	◯
The 8 in 2.083 is hundred times less than the 8 in 328.7	◯	◯
The 3 in 1.039 is hundred times less than the 3 in 67.3	◯	◯
The 2 in 9,523 is thousand times more than the 2 in 45.92	◯	◯

13. Fill in the blank.
The place value of the digit 3 in 67.039 is _____.

14. The digit 7 in which of the following numbers is hundred times more than the 7 in 539.7? Circle the correct answer choice

Ⓐ 172.43
Ⓑ 2728.4
Ⓒ 7426.1
Ⓓ 65.907

Name _____ Date _____

Chapter 3

Lesson 2: Multiplication & Division of Powers of Ten

You can scan the QR code given below or use the url to access additional EdSearch resources including videos and mobile apps related to *Multiplication & Division of Powers of Ten.*

 **Multiplication & Division of Powers of Ten**

URL	QR Code
http://www.lumoslearning.com/a/5nbta2	

1. Solve: $9 \times 10^3 =$

   Ⓐ 900
   Ⓑ 9,000
   Ⓒ 117
   Ⓓ 270

2. What is the quotient of 10^7 divided by 100?

   Ⓐ 0.7
   Ⓑ 100,000
   Ⓒ 70,000
   Ⓓ 700

3. Solve: $0.51 \times$ ____ $= 5,100$

   Ⓐ 10^4
   Ⓑ 10^2
   Ⓒ 100
   Ⓓ 10^3

4. Astronomers calculate a distant star to be 3×10^5 light years away. How far away is the star?

   Ⓐ 30,000 light years
   Ⓑ 3,000 light years
   Ⓒ 3,000,000 light years
   Ⓓ 300,000 light years

5. A scientist calculates the weight of a substance as $6.9 \div 10^4$ grams. What is the weight of the substance?

   Ⓐ 69,000 grams
   Ⓑ 69 milligrams
   Ⓒ 0.00069 grams
   Ⓓ 6.9 kilograms

6. Looking through a microscope, a doctor finds a germ that is 0.00000082 millimeters long. How can he write this number in his notes?

   Ⓐ 8.2×10^7
   Ⓑ $8.2 \div 10^7$
   Ⓒ $8.2 \times 10^{0.00001}$
   Ⓓ $8.2 \div 700$

7. Which of the following is 10^5 times greater than 0.016?

   Ⓐ 160
   Ⓑ 1,600
   Ⓒ 16.0
   Ⓓ 1.60

8. Find the missing number.
   _____ x 477 = 47,700,000

   Ⓐ 10,000,000
   Ⓑ 10 x 5
   Ⓒ 10^5
   Ⓓ 1,000

9. The number 113 is _____ times greater than 0.113.

   Ⓐ 3
   Ⓑ 10^3
   Ⓒ 30
   Ⓓ 10,000

10. _____ ÷ 10^5 = 4.6

   Ⓐ 460
   Ⓑ 4,600
   Ⓒ 46,000
   Ⓓ 460,000

11. Complete the table by writing the given number as a power of ten or the power of ten as a standard number.

1,000,000	
	10^4
100	
	10^7

12. Write the number 1,000 as a power of ten. Enter your answer in the box given below

```
┌─────────────────────────────┐
│                             │
│                             │
└─────────────────────────────┘
```

13. Circle the power of ten that represents 100,000,000.

Ⓐ 10^6
Ⓑ 10^8
Ⓒ 10^9
Ⓓ 10^{10}

Chapter 3

Lesson 3: Read and Write Decimals

You can scan the QR code given below or use the url to access additional EdSearch resources including videos and mobile apps related to *Read and Write Decimals*.

 **Read and Write Decimals**

URL	QR Code
http://www.lumoslearning.com/a/5nbta3	

1. **How is the number four hundredths written?**

    Ⓐ 0.04
    Ⓑ 0.400
    Ⓒ 400.0
    Ⓓ 0.004

2. **How is the number 0.2 read?**

    Ⓐ Zero and two
    Ⓑ Decimal two
    Ⓒ Two tenths
    Ⓓ Two hundredths

3. **What is the decimal form of $\frac{7}{10}$?**

    Ⓐ 7.10
    Ⓑ 0.7
    Ⓒ 10.7
    Ⓓ 0.07

4. **The number 0.05 can be represented by which fraction?**

    Ⓐ $\frac{0}{5}$

    Ⓑ $\frac{5}{100}$

    Ⓒ $\frac{5}{10}$

    Ⓓ $\frac{1}{05}$

5. **Which of the following numbers is equivalent to one half?**

    Ⓐ 0.2
    Ⓑ 0.12
    Ⓒ 1.2
    Ⓓ 0.5

6. **How is the number sixty three hundredths written?**

    Ⓐ 0.63
    Ⓑ 0.063
    Ⓒ 0.0063
    Ⓓ 6.300

7. **What is the correct way to read the number 40.057?**

   Ⓐ Forty point five seven
   Ⓑ Forty and fifty-seven hundredths
   Ⓒ Forty and fifty-seven thousandths
   Ⓓ Forty and five hundredths and seven thousandths

8. **Which of the following numbers has:**
   0 in the hundredths place
   8 in the tenths place
   3 in the thousandths place
   9 in the ones place

   Ⓐ 9.083
   Ⓑ 0.839
   Ⓒ 9.803
   Ⓓ 0.9803

9. **For which number is this the expanded form?**
   $9 \times 10 + 2 \times 1 + 3 \times (\frac{1}{10}) + 8 \times (\frac{1}{100})$

   Ⓐ 98.08
   Ⓑ 93.48
   Ⓒ 9.238
   Ⓓ 92.38

10. **What is the correct expanded form of the number 0.85?**

    Ⓐ $(8 \times 10) + (5 \times 100)$
    Ⓑ $8 \times (\frac{1}{10}) + 5 \times (\frac{1}{100})$
    Ⓒ $85 \div 10$
    Ⓓ $(8 \div 10) \times (5 \div 10)$

11. **Which of the following numbers are written correctly in expanded form? Note that more than one option may be correct. Select all the correct answers**

    Ⓐ $452.25 = 4 \times 100 + 5 \times 10 + 2 \times 1 + 1 + 5 \times 10$
    Ⓑ $53.81 = 5 \times 10 + 3 \times 1 + 8 \times (\frac{1}{10}) + 1 \times (\frac{1}{100})$
    Ⓒ $3.72 = 3 \times 1 + 7 \times (\frac{10}{1}) + 2 \times (\frac{100}{1})$
    Ⓓ $923.04 = 9 \times 100 + 2 \times 10 + 3 \times 1 + 4 \times (\frac{1}{100})$

12. Read the equations below and indicate whether they are true or false.

	True	False
345.3 = three hundred forty-five and three hundredths.	◯	◯
900 x 30 x 2 x 4 x($\frac{1}{10}$) x 7($\frac{1}{100}$)> Nine hundred thirty-two and four hundredths	◯	◯
604.2 = 600 x 4 x 2 x ($\frac{1}{100}$)	◯	◯
1.805 > One and ninety-two hundredths	◯	◯

13. What is the standard form of this number?
    Seventy-nine million, four hundred seventeen thousand, six hundred eight
    Enter your answer in the box given below

14. Which of the following represents four thousand sixty-two and thirteen hundredths?
    Circle the correct answer choice.

    Ⓐ 462.13
    Ⓑ 4,602.013
    Ⓒ 4,062.13
    Ⓓ 4620.13

Name _____   Date _____

Chapter 3

Lesson 4: Comparing and Ordering Decimals

You can scan the QR code given below or use the url to access additional EdSearch resources including videos and mobile apps related to *Comparing and Ordering Decimals*.

 **ed**)Search   **Comparing and Ordering Decimals**

URL	QR Code
http://www.lumoslearning.com/a/5nbta3	

1. **Which of the following numbers is the least?**
   0.04, 4.00, 0.40, 40.0

   Ⓐ 0.04
   Ⓑ 4.00
   Ⓒ 0.40
   Ⓓ 40.0

2. **Which of the following numbers is greatest?**
   0.125, 0.251, 0.512, 0.215

   Ⓐ 0.125
   Ⓑ 0.251
   Ⓒ 0.512
   Ⓓ 0.215

3. **Which of the following numbers is less than seven hundredths?**

   Ⓐ 0.072
   Ⓑ 0.60
   Ⓒ 0.058
   Ⓓ All of these

4. **Which of the following comparisons is correct?**

   Ⓐ 48.01 = 48.1
   Ⓑ 25.4 < 25.40
   Ⓒ 10.83 < 10.093
   Ⓓ 392.01 < 392.1

5. **Arrange these numbers in order from least to greatest:**
   1.02, 1.2, 1.12, 2.12

   Ⓐ 1.2, 1.12, 1.02, 2.12
   Ⓑ 2.12, 1.2, 1.12, 1.02
   Ⓒ 1.02, 1.12, 1.2, 2.12
   Ⓓ 1.12, 2.12, 1.02, 1.2

6. **Which of the following is true?**

   Ⓐ 3.21 > 32.1
   Ⓑ 32.12 > 312.12
   Ⓒ 32.12 > 3.212
   Ⓓ 212.3 < 21.32

7. **Arrange these numbers in order from greatest to least:**
    2.4, 2.04, 2.21, 2.20

    Ⓐ 2.4, 2.04, 2.21, 2.20
    Ⓑ 2.4, 2.21, 2.20, 2.04
    Ⓒ 2.21, 2.20, 2.4, 2.04
    Ⓓ 2.20, 2.4, 2.04, 2.21

8. **Which of the following numbers completes the sequence below?**
    4.17, _____, 4.19

    Ⓐ 4.18
    Ⓑ 4.81
    Ⓒ 5.17
    Ⓓ 4.27

9. **Which of the following comparisons is true?**

    Ⓐ 0.403 > 0.304
    Ⓑ 0.043 < 0.403
    Ⓒ 0.043 < 0.304
    Ⓓ All of the above

10. **Which number completes the following sequence?**
    2.038, 2.039, _____

    Ⓐ 2.049
    Ⓑ 2.400
    Ⓒ 2.0391
    Ⓓ 2.04

11. **Which of the following decimals is greater than 0.424 but less than 0.43.**
    Circle the correct answer choice

    Ⓐ 0.4
    Ⓑ 0.423
    Ⓒ 0.431
    Ⓓ 0.429

12. **Order the following numbers from least to greatest.**
   1.003, 0.853, 0.85, 1.03, 0.96, 0.921
   Enter your answers in the correct order in the boxes given below

Name _____ Date _____

Lesson 5: Rounding Decimals

You can scan the QR code given below or use the url to access additional EdSearch resources including videos and mobile apps related to *Rounding Decimals*.

 **Rounding Decimals**

URL	QR Code
http://www.lumoslearning.com/a/5nbta4	

1. **Is $7.48 closest to $6, $7 or $8?**

    Ⓐ $6
    Ⓑ $7
    Ⓒ $8
    Ⓓ It is right in the middle of $7 and $8

2. **Round the Olympic time of 56.389 seconds to the nearest tenth of a second.**

    Ⓐ 56.0
    Ⓑ 57
    Ⓒ 56.4
    Ⓓ 56.39

3. **Round the number 57.81492 to the nearest hundredth.**

    Ⓐ 57.82
    Ⓑ 58.00
    Ⓒ 57.80
    Ⓓ 57.81

4. **Which of the following numbers would round to 13.75?**

    Ⓐ 13.755
    Ⓑ 13.70
    Ⓒ 13.756
    Ⓓ 13.747

5. **Jerry spent $5.91, $7.27, and $12.60 on breakfast, lunch, and dinner. Approximately how much did his meals cost in all?**

    Ⓐ about $24
    Ⓑ about $26
    Ⓒ about $25
    Ⓓ about $27

6. **Maria needs to buy wood for a door frame. She needs two pieces that are 6.21 feet long and one piece that is 2.5 feet long. About how much wood should she buy?**

    Ⓐ about 15 feet
    Ⓑ about 9 feet
    Ⓒ about 17 feet
    Ⓓ about 14 feet

7. Mika has a rectangular flower garden. It measures 12.2 meters on one side and 7.8 meters on the other. What is a reasonable estimation of the area of the flower garden? (Area= length x width)

   Ⓐ 96 square meters
   Ⓑ 20 square meters
   Ⓒ 66 square meters
   Ⓓ 120 square meters

8. Shanda ran a lap in 6.78 minutes. Assuming she maintains this time for every lap she runs, estimate the time it would take her to run three laps.

   Ⓐ 25 minutes
   Ⓑ 21 minutes
   Ⓒ 18 minutes
   Ⓓ 10 minutes

9. A basketball player scores an average of 13.2 points per game. During a 62-game season, he would be expected to score about _____ points. (Assume he will play every game.)

   Ⓐ 600 points
   Ⓑ 1,000 points
   Ⓒ 800 points
   Ⓓ 400 points

10. Use estimation to complete the following:
    The difference of 31.245 - 1.396 is between _____.

    Ⓐ 29 and 29.5
    Ⓑ 29.5 and 30
    Ⓒ 30 and 30.5
    Ⓓ 30.5 and 31

11. When rounding to the nearest one's place, which of the following results in 430? More than one option may be correct. Select all the correct answers.

    Ⓐ 429.67
    Ⓑ 430.49
    Ⓒ 429.365
    Ⓓ 430.05

12. Read each statement below and mark the correct column to indicate whether you must round up or keep the digit.

	Round Up	Keep
Round 5.483 to the nearest hundredth.	○	○
Round 6.625 to the nearest tenth.	○	○
Round 77.951 to the nearest one.	○	○
Round 172.648 to the nearest hundredth.	○	○

13. Which of the following is rounded incorrectly?
Circle the correct answer choice.

Ⓐ 226.35 to the nearest tenth is 226.4.
Ⓑ 1,430.49 to the nearest one is 1,431.
Ⓒ 0.318 to the nearest tenth is 0.3.
Ⓓ 10.067 to the nearest hundredth is 10.07

Name _____   Date _____

Chapter 3

Lesson 6: Multiplication of Whole Numbers

You can scan the QR code given below or use the url to access additional EdSearch resources including videos and mobile apps related to *Multiplication of Whole Numbers*.

 Multiplication of Whole Numbers

URL	QR Code
http://www.lumoslearning.com/a/5nbtb5	

1. Solve. 79 x 14 = _____

   Ⓐ 790
   Ⓑ 1,106
   Ⓒ 854
   Ⓓ 224

2. A farmer plants 18 rows of beans. If there are 50 bean plants in each row, how many plants will he have altogether?

   Ⓐ 908
   Ⓑ 68
   Ⓒ 900
   Ⓓ 98

3. Solve. 680 x 94 = _____

   Ⓐ 64,070
   Ⓑ 63,960
   Ⓒ 64,760
   Ⓓ 63,920

4. What is the missing value?
   ____ x 11 = 374

   Ⓐ 36
   Ⓑ 30
   Ⓒ 34
   Ⓓ 31

5. Which of the following statements is true?

   Ⓐ 28 x 17 = 17 x 28
   Ⓑ 28 x 17 = 20 x 8 x 10 x 7
   Ⓒ 28 x 17 = (28 x 1) + (28 x 7)
   Ⓓ 28 x 17 = 27 x 18

6. **Which equation is represented by this array?**

- Ⓐ 3 + 7 + 3 + 7 = 20
- Ⓑ 7 + 7 + 7 + 7 + 7 = 35
- Ⓒ 3 x 3 + 7 = 16
- Ⓓ 3 x 7 = 21

7. **What would be a quick way to solve 596 x 101 accurately?**

- Ⓐ Multiply 5 x 101, 9 x 101, 6 x 101, then add the products.
- Ⓑ Multiply 596 x 100 then add 596 more.
- Ⓒ Shift the 1 and multiply 597 x 100 instead.
- Ⓓ Estimate 600 x 100.

8. **Harold baked 9 trays of cookies for a party. Three of the trays held 15 cookies each and six of the trays held 18 cookies each. How many cookies did Harold bake in all?**

- Ⓐ 297
- Ⓑ 135
- Ⓒ 153
- Ⓓ 162

9. **What's wrong with the following computation?**

```
        2 8
      x 5 3
    ---------
        3 2
        6 0
      4 0 0
  + 1 0 0 0
    ---------
    1 4 9 2
    ---------
```

- Ⓐ 3 x 8 is multiplied incorrectly.
- Ⓑ 50 x 20 should only have two zeros.
- Ⓒ 5 x 8 is only 40.
- Ⓓ There's a missing 1 that should have been carried from the tens to the hundreds place.

10. Solve.
407 x 35 = _____

Ⓐ 14,280
Ⓑ 14,245
Ⓒ 12,445
Ⓓ 16,135

11. Find the product.
673 x 14 = _____

12. What is the product of 1620 x 944.
Circle the correct answer choice.

Ⓐ 27,540
Ⓑ 1,529,280
Ⓒ 217,080
Ⓓ 942,180

13. Callie is calculating the product of 268 x 5,321. Help her complete the table below.

268	×	1	=	268
268	×		=	5,360
	×	300	=	80,400
268	×		=	
	×	Total	=	

14. What is the product of 321 X 1854
Enter your answer in the box given below.

Chapter 3

Lesson 7: Division of Whole Numbers

You can scan the QR code given below or use the url to access additional EdSearch resources including videos and mobile apps related to *Division of Whole Numbers*.

 **Division of Whole Numbers**

URL	QR Code
http://www.lumoslearning.com/a/5nbtb6	

1. Find the missing number:
    48 ÷ ___ = 12

    Ⓐ 4
    Ⓑ 10
    Ⓒ 6
    Ⓓ 8

2. Hannah is filling gift bags for a party. She has 72 pieces of candy to pass out. If there are 8 bags, how many pieces of candy will go in each bag?

    Ⓐ 8
    Ⓑ 10
    Ⓒ 9
    Ⓓ 7

3. Solve. 1,248 ÷ 6 =

    Ⓐ 2,080
    Ⓑ 208
    Ⓒ 28
    Ⓓ 280

4. The fifth grade class took a field trip to the theater. The 96 students sat in rows with 10 students in each row. How many rows did they use?

    Ⓐ 11
    Ⓑ 9
    Ⓒ 10
    Ⓓ 12

5. What is the value of 6,720 ÷ 15?

    Ⓐ 510
    Ⓑ 426
    Ⓒ 448
    Ⓓ 528

6   What is 675,000 divided by 100?

    Ⓐ 675
    Ⓑ 67,500
    Ⓒ 67.5
    Ⓓ 6,750

7. **Which of the following statements is true?**

   (A) $75 \div 0 = 0$
   (B) $75 \div 0 = 1$
   (C) $75 \div 0 = 75$
   (D) $75 \div 0$ cannot be solved

8. **Taylor is putting 100 donuts into boxes. Each box holds 12 donuts. How many donuts will be left over after filling the last box fully?**

   (A) 4
   (B) 8
   (C) 9
   (D) 5

9. **Which of the following statements is true?**

   (A) $26 \div 1 = 1$
   (B) $26 \div 1 = 26$
   (C) $26 \div 1 = 0$
   (D) $26 \div 1$ cannot be solved

10. **Jeremy is rolling coins to take to the bank. He has 680 nickels to roll. If each sleeve holds 40 nickels, how many sleeves will he be able to fill?**

    (A) 8
    (B) 17
    (C) 16
    (D) 12

11. **Which of the following equations is true? Select the two correct answers.**

    (A) $432 \div 12 = 36$
    (B) $432 \div 8 = 44$
    (C) $432 \div 18 = 24$
    (D) $432 \div 16 = 30$

12. Read the following math sentences and indicate which are true and which are false.

	True	False
385 ÷ 35 > 12	○	○
1,680 ÷ 48 = 35	○	○
4,088 ÷ 56 = 75	○	○
884 ÷ 26 < 36	○	○

13. Which of the following completes the equation 564 ÷ _____ = 47
    Circle the correct answer choice

    Ⓐ 13
    Ⓑ 18
    Ⓒ 12
    Ⓓ 28

14. Divide 388 by 15.
    Enter the answer in the box given below

15. 6,720 ÷ 15 = _____

Chapter 3

Lesson 8: Add, Subtract, Multiply, & Divide Decimals

You can scan the QR code given below or use the url to access additional EdSearch resources including videos and mobile apps related to *Add, Subtract, Multiply, & Divide Decimals*.

 Add, Subtract, Multiply, & Divide Decimals

URL	QR Code
http://www.lumoslearning.com/a/5nbtb7	

1. At a math competition, three members of a team each solved a problem as quickly as they could. Their times were 4.18 seconds, 3.75 seconds, and 3.99 seconds. What was the total of their times?

Ⓐ 11.92 seconds
Ⓑ 10.99 seconds
Ⓒ 10.72 seconds
Ⓓ 11.72 seconds

2. Beginning with the number 6.472, add:
   1 hundredth
   3 ones
   5 tenths
   What is the result?

Ⓐ 7.822
Ⓑ 6.823
Ⓒ 9.982
Ⓓ 6.607

3. Find the perimeter (total length of all four sides) of a trapezoid whose sides measure 2.09 ft, 2.09 ft, 3.72 ft, and 6.60 ft.

Ⓐ 16.12 ft
Ⓑ 14.5 ft
Ⓒ 13.50 ft
Ⓓ 8.56 ft

4. Find the difference:
   85.37 - 75.2 =

Ⓐ 160.57
Ⓑ 10
Ⓒ 10.35
Ⓓ 10.17

5. Subtract:
   3.64 - 1.46 =

Ⓐ 2.18
Ⓑ 4.18
Ⓒ 1.18
Ⓓ 4.20

6. Normal body temperature is 98.6 degrees Fahrenheit. When Tyler had a fever, his temperature went up to 102.2 degrees. By how much did Tyler's temperature increase?

Ⓐ 4.4 degrees
Ⓑ 3.6 degrees
Ⓒ 4.2 degrees
Ⓓ 3.2 degrees

7. A stamp costs $0.42. How much money would you need to buy 8 stamps?

Ⓐ $.82
Ⓑ $3.33
Ⓒ $3.36
Ⓓ $4.52

8. Find the product:
   $0.25 \times 1.1 =$

Ⓐ .75
Ⓑ 0.275
Ⓒ 0.27
Ⓓ .25

9. Divide 0.42 by 3.

Ⓐ 14
Ⓑ 126
Ⓒ 0.14
Ⓓ 12.6

10. Solve:
    $0.09 \div 0.3 =$

Ⓐ 0.27
Ⓑ 0.003
Ⓒ 0.027
Ⓓ 0.3

11. Circle the number that is 5.47 more than 12.83 + 45.7

Ⓐ 68.53
Ⓑ 62.137
Ⓒ 64
Ⓓ 57.9

12. Solve:
    12.3 - 1.99 = _____

13. What decimal completes the equation in the table?
    Complete the table

3.5	×	4.01	=	

14. Solve:
    0.05 ÷ 0.2
    Enter your answer in the box below.

End of Numbers and Operations in Base Ten

Name _____ **Date** _____

Chapter 4:
Number & Operations - Fractions

Lesson 1: Add & Subtract Fractions

You can scan the QR code given below or use the url to access additional EdSearch resources including videos and mobile apps related to *Add & Subtract Fractions*.

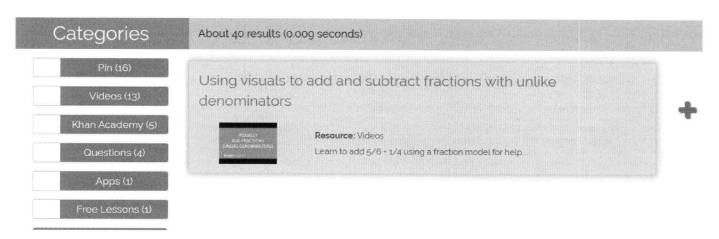

Categories	About 40 results (0.009 seconds)
Pin (16)	Using visuals to add and subtract fractions with unlike denominators
Videos (13)	
Khan Academy (5)	**Resource:** Videos
Questions (4)	Learn to add 5/6 + 1/4 using a fraction model for help...
Apps (1)	
Free Lessons (1)	

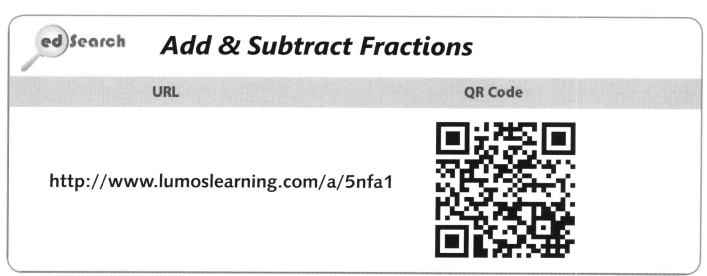

ed)Search   *Add & Subtract Fractions*

URL	QR Code
http://www.lumoslearning.com/a/5nfa1	

1. Add: $\dfrac{2}{10} + \dfrac{1}{10} =$

   Ⓐ $\dfrac{3}{20}$

   Ⓑ $\dfrac{3}{10}$

   Ⓒ $\dfrac{1}{10}$

   Ⓓ $\dfrac{2}{10}$

2. To make a bowl of punch, Joe mixed $1\dfrac{1}{4}$ gallons of juice with $1\dfrac{2}{4}$ gallons of sparkling water. How much punch does he have?

   Ⓐ $2\dfrac{3}{4}$ gallons

   Ⓑ 3 gallons

   Ⓒ $\dfrac{1}{4}$ gallon

   Ⓓ $\dfrac{3}{4}$ gallon

3. Subtract: $\dfrac{3}{4} - \dfrac{2}{4} =$

   Ⓐ $\dfrac{5}{4}$

   Ⓑ $\dfrac{1}{4}$

   Ⓒ $\dfrac{3}{4}$

   Ⓓ 1

4. Subtract: $3\dfrac{4}{10} - 1\dfrac{1}{10} =$

   Ⓐ $1\dfrac{3}{10}$

   Ⓑ $2\dfrac{1}{10}$

   Ⓒ $3\dfrac{3}{10}$

   Ⓓ $2\dfrac{3}{10}$

5. To add the fractions $\frac{3}{4}$ and $\frac{7}{12}$, what must first be done?

   Ⓐ Reduce the fractions to lowest terms
   Ⓑ Change to improper fractions
   Ⓒ Make the numerators the same
   Ⓓ Find a common denominator

6. Add: $\frac{1}{2} + \frac{1}{4} =$

   Ⓐ $\frac{2}{6}$

   Ⓑ $\frac{2}{3}$

   Ⓒ $\frac{3}{4}$

   Ⓓ $\frac{1}{2}$

7. Find the difference: $\frac{2}{3} - \frac{1}{9} =$

   Ⓐ $\frac{1}{6}$

   Ⓑ $\frac{5}{9}$

   Ⓒ $\frac{3}{12}$

   Ⓓ $\frac{2}{27}$

8. Find the sum: $2\frac{1}{8} + 5\frac{1}{2} =$

   Ⓐ $7\frac{2}{10}$

   Ⓑ $10\frac{1}{16}$

   Ⓒ $3\frac{1}{6}$

   Ⓓ $7\frac{5}{8}$

9. Find the sum of five and five eighths plus one and one fourth.

    Ⓐ $6\frac{7}{8}$

    Ⓑ $10\frac{6}{8}$

    Ⓒ $6\frac{6}{12}$

    Ⓓ $7\frac{2}{10}$

10. Subtract: $5 - \frac{1}{3} =$

    Ⓐ $5\frac{1}{3}$

    Ⓑ $4\frac{1}{3}$

    Ⓒ $3\frac{2}{3}$

    Ⓓ $4\frac{2}{3}$

11. Jordan had a plank of wood that was $8\frac{5}{16}$ inches long. He sawed off $2\frac{3}{16}$ inches. Now how long is the plank of wood?

    Ⓐ $10\frac{8}{32}$ inches

    Ⓑ $6\frac{1}{4}$ inches

    Ⓒ $6\frac{2}{16}$ inches

    Ⓓ $10\frac{8}{16}$ inches

12. At the beginning of 5th grade, Amber's hair was $8\frac{1}{2}$ inches long. By the end of 5th grade it was $10\frac{3}{4}$ inches long. How many inches did Amber's hair grow during 5th grade?

    Ⓐ $19\frac{1}{4}$ inches

    Ⓑ $18\frac{4}{6}$ inches

    Ⓒ $2\frac{1}{2}$ inches

    Ⓓ $2\frac{1}{4}$ inches

13. Solve: $\dfrac{1}{5} + \dfrac{3}{5} + \dfrac{4}{5} =$ _____

14. Find the missing number: $4\dfrac{1}{4} +$ _____ $= 7\dfrac{1}{2}$

Ⓐ $3\dfrac{1}{4}$

Ⓑ $3\dfrac{3}{4}$

Ⓒ $3\dfrac{1}{2}$

Ⓓ $2\dfrac{3}{4}$

15. Solve: $\dfrac{7}{10} - \left(\dfrac{4}{10} - \dfrac{1}{10}\right) =$

Ⓐ $\dfrac{2}{10}$

Ⓑ $\dfrac{4}{10}$

Ⓒ 0

Ⓓ $\dfrac{3}{10}$

16. Which of the following expression(s) is equivalent to $\dfrac{2}{3} + \dfrac{7}{4}$?
Select all the correct answers

Ⓐ $\dfrac{4}{6} + \dfrac{9}{6}$

Ⓑ $\dfrac{8}{12} + \dfrac{21}{12}$

Ⓒ $\dfrac{40}{60} + \dfrac{105}{60}$

Ⓓ $\dfrac{12}{16} + \dfrac{28}{16}$

Ⓒ $\dfrac{20}{36} + \dfrac{54}{36}$

17. What is the value of $\dfrac{3}{5} - \dfrac{2}{7}$

   Write your answer in the box given below

Chapter 4

Lesson 2: Problem Solving with Fractions

You can scan the QR code given below or use the url to access additional EdSearch resources including videos and mobile apps related to *Problem Solving with Fractions*.

 Problem Solving with Fractions

URL	QR Code
http://www.lumoslearning.com/a/5nfa2	

Name _____   Date _____

1. Susan's homework was to practice the piano for $\dfrac{3}{4}$ of an hour each night. How many minutes each night did she practice?

Ⓐ 30 minutes
Ⓑ 15 minutes
Ⓒ 45 minutes
Ⓓ 60 minutes

2. Three fifths of the 30 students are boys. How many students are girls?

Ⓐ 12 girls
Ⓑ 18 girls
Ⓒ 6 girls
Ⓓ 8 girls

3. Walking at a steady pace, Ella walked 11 miles in 3 hours. Which mixed number shows how many miles she walked in an hour?

Ⓐ $\dfrac{2}{3}$
Ⓑ $2\dfrac{2}{3}$
Ⓒ 3
Ⓓ $3\dfrac{2}{3}$

4. In science class we discovered that $\dfrac{7}{8}$ of an apple is water. What fraction of the apple is not water?

Ⓐ $\dfrac{1}{6}$
Ⓑ $\dfrac{1}{7}$
Ⓒ $\dfrac{7}{8}$
Ⓓ $\dfrac{1}{8}$

5. There were 20 pumpkins in a garden. One fourth of the pumpkins were too small, one tenth were too large, and one half were just the right size. The rest were not ripe yet. How many of the pumpkins were too small?

Ⓐ 3
Ⓑ 2
Ⓒ 5
Ⓓ 10

6. Timothy decided to clean out his closet by donating some of his 45 button-down shirts. He gave away 9 shirts. What fraction of the shirts did he give away?

   Ⓐ $\dfrac{1}{5}$

   Ⓑ $\dfrac{1}{9}$

   Ⓒ $\dfrac{1}{2}$

   Ⓓ $\dfrac{36}{45}$

7. There are 32 students in Mr. Duffy's class. If 4 come to after school tutoring, what fraction of the class comes to after school tutoring?

   Ⓐ $\dfrac{28}{32}$

   Ⓑ $\dfrac{1}{8}$

   Ⓒ $\dfrac{1}{4}$

   Ⓓ $\dfrac{2}{8}$

8. Dara has to solve 35 math problems for homework. She has completed 14 of them. What fraction of the problems does she have left to do?

   Ⓐ $\dfrac{14}{35}$

   Ⓑ $\dfrac{3}{5}$

   Ⓒ $\dfrac{14}{21}$

   Ⓓ $\dfrac{2}{5}$

9. A 5th grade volleyball team scored 32 points in one game. Of those points, $\dfrac{2}{8}$ were scored in the second half. How many points were scored in the first half of the game?

   Ⓐ 12
   Ⓑ 4
   Ⓒ 20
   Ⓓ 24

10. A recipe to make 48 cookies calls for 3 cups of flour. However, you do not want to make 48 cookies, but only 24 cookies. Which fraction shows how much flour to use?

Ⓐ 2 cups

Ⓑ $1\frac{2}{3}$ cups

Ⓒ $1\frac{1}{2}$ cups

Ⓓ $2\frac{2}{3}$ cups

11. Match the statement with the symbol that will make the statement true

	>	<	=
$\frac{5}{6} - \frac{2}{3} \Box \frac{1}{2} - \frac{3}{8}$	○	○	○
$\frac{5}{6} + \frac{2}{3} \Box \frac{3}{4} + \frac{5}{12}$	○	○	○
$\frac{3}{15} + \frac{2}{5} \Box \frac{1}{3} + \frac{2}{5}$	○	○	○
$\frac{7}{8} - \frac{1}{4} \Box \frac{3}{4} - \frac{1}{8}$	○	○	○

12. A recipe calls for $\frac{1}{2}$ pound of butter. If there is $\frac{5}{8}$ of a pound, how much (pounds) of butter is left after the cooking? Circle the correct answer.

Ⓐ $\frac{1}{8}$

Ⓑ $\frac{5}{4}$

Ⓒ $\frac{2}{3}$

Ⓓ $\frac{5}{16}$

13. Forest bought a can of paint to paint his drone. If the first coat of paint used $\frac{2}{3}$ of the can of paint and the second coat used $\frac{2}{15}$ of the can, select the correct equation to determine the fraction of the paint used on the drone? Circle on the correct answer.

Ⓐ $\frac{2}{15} - \frac{2}{3} = \frac{2}{15} - \frac{10}{15} = -\frac{8}{15}$

Ⓑ $\frac{2}{3} + \frac{2}{5} = \frac{10}{15} + \frac{2}{15} = \frac{12}{15} = \frac{4}{5}$

Ⓒ $\frac{2}{3} - \frac{2}{15} = \frac{10}{15} - \frac{2}{15} = \frac{(10-2)}{15} = \frac{8}{15}$

Ⓓ $\frac{2}{3} \times \frac{2}{15} = \frac{4}{45}$

Chapter 4

Lesson 3: Interpreting Fractions

You can scan the QR code given below or use the url to access additional EdSearch resources including videos and mobile apps related to *Interpreting Fractions*.

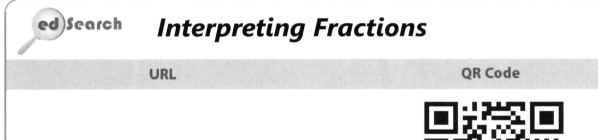

ed Search   *Interpreting Fractions*

URL	QR Code
http://www.lumoslearning.com/a/5nfb3	

1. Suppose three friends wanted to share four cookies equally. How many cookies would each friend receive?

   Ⓐ $1\dfrac{1}{3}$

   Ⓑ $\dfrac{3}{4}$

   Ⓒ $1\dfrac{3}{4}$

   Ⓓ $\dfrac{1}{3}$

2. If 18 is divided by 5, which fraction represents the remainder divided by divisor?

   Ⓐ $\dfrac{3}{18}$

   Ⓑ $\dfrac{3}{5}$

   Ⓒ $\dfrac{5}{18}$

   Ⓓ $\dfrac{1}{3}$

3. If there are 90 minutes in a soccer game and 4 squads of players will share this time equally, how many minutes will each squad play?

   Ⓐ $\dfrac{22}{4}$

   Ⓑ $22\dfrac{1}{2}$

   Ⓒ $22\dfrac{2}{10}$

   Ⓓ $18\dfrac{4}{22}$

4. Damien has $695 in the bank. He wants to withdraw $\dfrac{2}{5}$th of his money. If he uses a calculator to figure out this amount, which buttons should he press?

   Ⓐ [6] [9] [5] [x] [2] [x] [5] [=]
   Ⓑ [6] [9] [5] [÷] [2] [x] [5] [=]
   Ⓒ [6] [9] [5] [÷] [2] [÷] [5] [=]
   Ⓓ [6] [9] [5] [x] [2] [÷] [5] [=]

5. **Five friends are taking a trip in a car. They want to share the driving equally. If the trip takes 7 hours, how long should each friend drive?**

Ⓐ $\dfrac{5}{7}$ of an hour

Ⓑ 1 hour 7 minutes

Ⓒ $1\dfrac{2}{5}$ hours

Ⓓ 1 hour 2 minutes

6. **Which fraction is equivalent to 3 ÷ 10?**

Ⓐ $\dfrac{1}{3}$

Ⓑ $\dfrac{10}{3}$

Ⓒ $\dfrac{13}{3}$

Ⓓ $\dfrac{3}{10}$

7. **Which number completes this equation?**
$$\dfrac{5}{8} = 5 \div \underline{\quad}$$

Ⓐ 13

Ⓑ $\dfrac{1}{5}$

Ⓒ 8

Ⓓ $\dfrac{1}{8}$

8. **If 9 people want to share a birthday cake equally, what fraction of the cake will each person get?**

Ⓐ $\dfrac{8}{9}$

Ⓑ $\dfrac{1}{9}$

Ⓒ $\dfrac{1}{2}$

Ⓓ $\dfrac{9}{2}$

9. Which number completes this equation?

$$\frac{4}{7} \times 7 = \underline{}$$

Ⓐ 4

Ⓑ 28

Ⓒ $\frac{4}{49}$

Ⓓ $\frac{21}{7}$

10. Which number completes this equation?

$$\frac{2}{3} = \underline{} \div 3$$

Ⓐ 3

Ⓑ $\frac{1}{2}$

Ⓒ 2

Ⓓ $\frac{1}{3}$

11. Sinclair made 6 points out of the team's total of 24 points. What fraction of the team's total points did Sinclair make? Select all the correct answers.

Ⓐ $\frac{2}{5}$

Ⓑ $\frac{6}{24}$

Ⓒ $\frac{1}{4}$

Ⓓ $\frac{2}{6}$

12. Justine found 6-feet of string with which to make 8 bracelets. If each bracelet was the same length, how long was each bracelet? Enter your answer in the box as a fraction in its simplest form.

Chapter 4

Lesson 4: Multiply Fractions

You can scan the QR code given below or use the url to access additional EdSearch resources including videos and mobile apps related to *Multiply Fractions*.

 **Multiply Fractions**

URL	QR Code
http://www.lumoslearning.com/a/5nfb4	

1. Multiply: $\dfrac{2}{3}$ x $\dfrac{4}{5}$ =

Ⓐ $\dfrac{8}{15}$

Ⓑ $\dfrac{3}{4}$

Ⓒ $\dfrac{6}{8}$

Ⓓ $\dfrac{4}{15}$

2. Find the product: 5 x $\dfrac{2}{3}$ x $\dfrac{1}{2}$ =

Ⓐ $1\dfrac{1}{3}$

Ⓑ 5

Ⓒ $2\dfrac{2}{3}$

Ⓓ $1\dfrac{2}{3}$

3. Which of the following is equivalent to $\dfrac{5}{6}$ x 7?

Ⓐ 5 ÷ (6 x 7)

Ⓑ (5 x 7) ÷ 6

Ⓒ (6 x 7) ÷ 5

Ⓓ (1 ÷ 7) x (5 ÷ 6)

4. Which of the following is equivalent to $\dfrac{4}{10}$ x $\dfrac{3}{8}$?

Ⓐ 4 ÷ (10 x 3) ÷ 8

Ⓑ (4 + 3) x (10 + 8)

Ⓒ (4 x 3) ÷ (10 x 8)

Ⓓ (4 - 3) ÷ (10 - 8)

5. Hector is using wood to build a dog house. Each wall is $\dfrac{4}{7}$ of a yard tall and $\dfrac{3}{5}$ of a yard wide. Knowing that the area of each wall is the base times the height, how many square yards of wood will he need to build 4 walls of equal size?

Ⓐ $1\dfrac{2}{3}$

Ⓑ $1\dfrac{13}{35}$

Ⓒ $\dfrac{12}{35}$

Ⓓ $1\dfrac{4}{12}$

6. **An auditorium has 600 seats. One-third of the seats are empty. How many seats are empty?**

    Ⓐ 300 seats
    Ⓑ 400 seats
    Ⓒ 200 seats
    Ⓓ 900 seats

7. **Which of these numbers is not equivalent to the other three?**

    Ⓐ $\dfrac{44}{8}$

    Ⓑ $5\dfrac{25}{50}$

    Ⓒ $5\dfrac{1}{5}$

    Ⓓ 5.500

8. **Multiply:** $\dfrac{1}{2} \times \dfrac{1}{4} =$

    Ⓐ $\dfrac{1}{2}$

    Ⓑ $\dfrac{1}{8}$

    Ⓒ $\dfrac{2}{8}$

    Ⓓ $2\dfrac{1}{2}$

9. **What fraction is one half of three fourths?**

    Ⓐ $\dfrac{1}{3}$

    Ⓑ $\dfrac{3}{4}$

    Ⓒ $\dfrac{3}{8}$

    Ⓓ $\dfrac{1}{8}$

10. One half of one tenth is what fraction?

Ⓐ $\dfrac{1}{5}$

Ⓑ $\dfrac{1}{20}$

Ⓒ $\dfrac{1}{10}$

Ⓓ $\dfrac{1}{2}$

11. Read each equation below and mark the box to indicate whether the equation is true or false.

	True	False
$4 \times \dfrac{3}{4} = 3$	○	○
$\dfrac{1}{6}$ of 7 is $\dfrac{6}{7}$	○	○
$\dfrac{1}{3} \times 9 = 3$	○	○
$10 \times \dfrac{1}{6} = 1\dfrac{2}{3}$	○	○

12. Fill in the table to complete the math sentence.

$\dfrac{1}{6}$	×		=	$\dfrac{3}{24}$	=	

13. Terry brought some chocolate for lunch and shared it evenly among himself and two friends. If his share was $\frac{1}{6}$ of a pound, how much chocolate did Terry bring to school? Circle the correct answer choice

(A)

(B)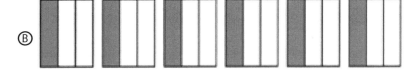

(C)

(D)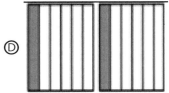

Chapter 4

Lesson 5: Multiply to Find Area

You can scan the QR code given below or use the url to access additional EdSearch resources including videos and mobile apps related to *Multiply to Find Area*.

 **Multiply to Find Area**

URL	QR Code
http://www.lumoslearning.com/a/5nfb4b	

1. Dominique is covering the top of her desk with contact paper. The surface measures $\frac{7}{8}$ yard by $\frac{3}{4}$ yard. How much contact paper will she need to cover the surface of the desktop?

   Ⓐ $\frac{21}{32}$ yd²

   Ⓑ $\frac{13}{8}$ yd²

   Ⓒ $\frac{20}{24}$ yd²

   Ⓓ $1\frac{5}{8}$ yd²

2. Christopher is tiling his bathroom floor with tiles that are each 1 square foot. The floor measures $2\frac{1}{2}$ feet by $3\frac{3}{4}$ feet. How many tiles will he need to cover the floor?

   Ⓐ $6\frac{3}{8}$

   Ⓑ $6\frac{1}{4}$

   Ⓒ $9\frac{3}{8}$

   Ⓓ 8

3. Lin and Tyra are measuring the area of the piece of paper shown below. Lin multiplied the length times the width to find an answer. Tyra traced the paper onto 1-inch graph paper and counted the number of squares. How should their answers compare?

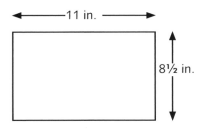

11 in.

8½ in.

   Ⓐ Lin's answer will be a mixed number, but Tyra's will be a whole number.
   Ⓑ Tyra's answer will be greater than Lin's answer.
   Ⓒ Lin's answer will be greater than Tyra's answer.
   Ⓓ They should end up with almost exactly the same answer.

4. Jeremy found that it takes 14 centimeter cubes to cover the surface of a rectangular image. Which of these measurements could possibly be the length and width of the rectangle he covered? Assume that centimeter cubes can be cut so that fractional measurements are possible.

(A) Length = $3\frac{1}{2}$ cm, width = 4 cm

(B) Length = $4\frac{1}{2}$ cm, width = 3 cm

(C) Length = 7 cm, width = 7 cm

(D) Length = 7 cm, width = 3 cm

5. What is the area of the court shown below?

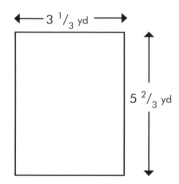

$\leftarrow$ $3\frac{1}{3}$ yd $\rightarrow$

$5\frac{2}{3}$ yd

(A) $15\frac{2}{9}$ yd²

(B) $18\frac{8}{9}$ yd²

(C) 16 yd²

(D) 9 yd²

6. A rectangle has a width of $\frac{3}{5}$ and a length of $\frac{4}{9}$. Choose two of the following answers that correctly represent the area of the rectangle?

(A) $\frac{47}{45}$

(B) $\frac{12}{45}$

(C) $\frac{1}{2}$

(D) $\frac{4}{15}$

7. **Use the picture below to find the area of the rectangle. Enter your answer in the box.**

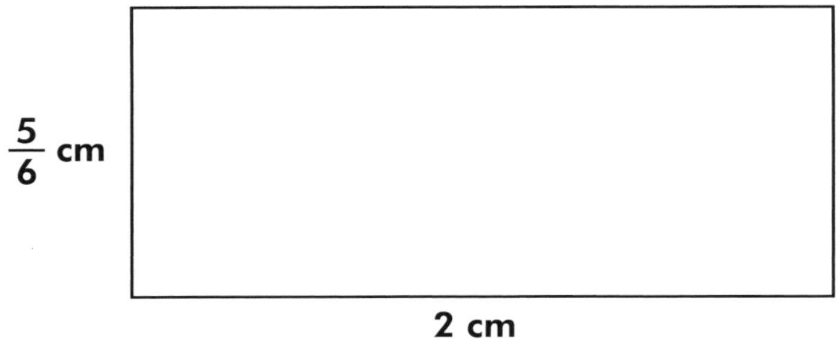

$\frac{5}{6}$ cm

2 cm

8. **Which of the following have an area less than one meter squared? Circle the correct answer choice.**

Ⓐ Length = $1\frac{3}{8}$ m; Width = $\frac{7}{9}$ sq m

Ⓑ Length = $2\frac{1}{6}$ m; Width = $\frac{3}{4}$ sq m

Ⓒ Length = $2\frac{5}{6}$ m; Width = $\frac{1}{3}$ sq m

Ⓓ Length = $1\frac{7}{8}$ m; Width = $\frac{4}{5}$ sq m

Name _____   **Date** _____

9. **Find the area of the rectangle**

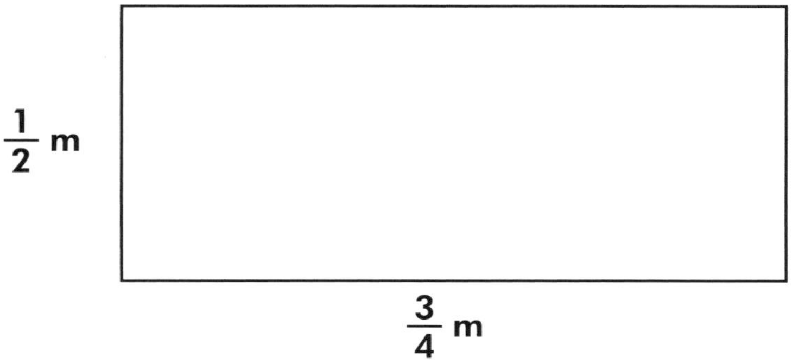

$\frac{1}{2}$ m

$\frac{3}{4}$ m

10. **Evaluate** $\frac{7}{12}$ x $\frac{1}{2}$

Ⓐ $\frac{7}{24}$

Ⓑ $\frac{7}{6}$

Ⓒ $\frac{6}{7}$

Ⓓ $\frac{1}{7}$

Chapter 4

Lesson 6: Multiplication as Scaling

You can scan the QR code given below or use the url to access additional EdSearch resources including videos and mobile apps related to *Multiplication as Scaling*.

 **Multiplication as Scaling**

URL	QR Code
http://www.lumoslearning.com/a/5nfb5a	

1. If y is four times as much as z, which number completes this equation?
   z * ___ = y

   Ⓐ 4
   Ⓑ 0.4
   Ⓒ $\dfrac{1}{4}$
   Ⓓ 40

2. In the equation a * b = c, if b is a fraction greater than 1, then c will be _____.

   Ⓐ a mixed number
   Ⓑ less than b
   Ⓒ greater than a
   Ⓓ equal to b ÷ 10

3. If d * e = f, and e is a fraction less than 1, then f will be _____.

   Ⓐ greater than d
   Ⓑ less than d
   Ⓒ equal to e ÷ d
   Ⓓ less than 1

4. In which equation is r less than s?

   Ⓐ r - 6 = s
   Ⓑ s * 6 = r
   Ⓒ r ÷ 6 = s
   Ⓓ s * $\dfrac{1}{6}$ = r

5. Ryan and Alex are using beads to make necklaces. Ryan used one fifth as many beads as Alex. Which equation is true?
   (Take R = Number of beads used by Ryan, A = Number of beads used by Alex).

   Ⓐ R * $\dfrac{1}{5}$ = A
   Ⓑ R = A * 5
   Ⓒ R * 5 = A
   Ⓓ R ÷ 5 = A

6. **Which statement is true about this equation?**
    5 x t = u

    Ⓐ t divided by u equals 5
    Ⓑ t plus 5 equals u
    Ⓒ u times 5 equals t
    Ⓓ t is $\frac{1}{5}$th of u

7. **f is 100 times as much as g when:**

    Ⓐ g x 100 = f
    Ⓑ g + 100 = f
    Ⓒ f x 10 = g
    Ⓓ $\frac{1}{10}$ of f = g

8. **When multiplying 82 x 25, the product will be _____.**

    Ⓐ less than 10 times 82
    Ⓑ 100 times as much as 25
    Ⓒ 25 times as much as 82
    Ⓓ equal to 82 divided by 25

9. **In the equation 19 x 78 = m, which of the following is true?**

    Ⓐ m is 78 times as much as 19
    Ⓑ m is 19 times less than 78
    Ⓒ m is equal to 78 divided by 19
    Ⓓ m is 78 more than 19

10. **If j is three hundred times as much as k, which number completes this equation?**
    k x ___ = j

    Ⓐ $\frac{1}{30}$
    Ⓑ 300
    Ⓒ (3 + 100)
    Ⓓ 0.03

11. Read each comparison and indicate whether the comparison is true or false

	True	False
$\dfrac{7}{8} \times \dfrac{3}{4} > \dfrac{7}{8}$	○	○
$2\dfrac{1}{2} \times \dfrac{6}{5} < 2\dfrac{1}{2}$	○	○
$\dfrac{8}{15} \times \dfrac{1}{3} < \dfrac{1}{3}$	○	○
$\dfrac{11}{12} \times \dfrac{3}{2} < \dfrac{11}{12}$	○	○

12. Circle the fraction that will complete the statement below:

3 x ? > 3

Ⓐ $\dfrac{2}{3}$

Ⓑ $\dfrac{7}{8}$

Ⓒ $\dfrac{6}{5}$

Ⓓ $\dfrac{3}{4}$

13. Enter <1 or >1 into the table below to complete a true comparison.

$\dfrac{8}{9}$	×		<	$\dfrac{8}{9}$
	×	$1\dfrac{1}{5}$	<	$1\dfrac{1}{5}$
$\dfrac{5}{4}$	×		>	$\dfrac{5}{4}$

Chapter 4

Lesson 7: Numbers Multiplied by Fractions

You can scan the QR code given below or use the url to access additional EdSearch resources including videos and mobile apps related to *Numbers Multiplied by Fractions*.

 **Numbers Multiplied by Fractions**

URL	QR Code
http://www.lumoslearning.com/a/5nfb5b	

1. **Which statement is true about the following equation?**
   $6,827 \times \dfrac{2}{7} = ?$

   Ⓐ The product will be less than 6,827.
   Ⓑ The product will be greater than 6,827.
   Ⓒ The product will be less than $\dfrac{2}{7}$.
   Ⓓ The product will be equal to $6,827 \div 7$.

2. **Which statement is true about the following equation?**
   $27,093 \times \dfrac{5}{4} = ?$

   Ⓐ The product will be equal to $27,093 \div 54$.
   Ⓑ The product will be less than $\dfrac{5}{4}$.
   Ⓒ The product will be less than 27,093.
   Ⓓ The product will be greater than 27,093.

3. **Estimate the product:**
   $18,612 \times 1\dfrac{1}{7} =$ _____

4. **Which number completes the equation?**
   $3,606 \times$ ___ $= 4,808$
   Enter your answer in the box given below

   ┌─────────────────────────────┐
   │   │
   │   │
   │   │
   └─────────────────────────────┘

5. **Which number completes the equation?**
   ___ $\times \dfrac{5}{6} = 17,365$

   Ⓐ 5,838
   Ⓑ 50,838
   Ⓒ 20,838
   Ⓓ 10,838

6. When 6 is multiplied by the following fractions, which of the products will be greater than 6? Select all the correct answers.

Ⓐ $\frac{4}{5}$

Ⓑ $\frac{10}{9}$

Ⓒ $\frac{3}{2}$

Ⓓ $\frac{13}{14}$

7. Write the correct comparison symbol that best completes the statement.

Ⓐ $5 \times \frac{2}{3}$ ☐ 5

Ⓑ $\frac{4}{3} \times 8$ ☐ 8

Ⓒ $12 \times \frac{4}{7}$ ☐ 12

Ⓓ $4 \times \frac{24}{24}$ ☐ 4

8. Which of the following expressions is true.

Ⓐ $25 \times \frac{6}{7} > 25$

Ⓑ $\frac{4}{3} \times 43 < 43$

Ⓒ $\frac{9}{15} \times 16 < 16$

Ⓓ $59 \times \frac{19}{20} > 59$

9. Compare using < , > or =

44 ☐ $44 \times \frac{3}{4}$

Ⓐ <

Ⓑ >

Ⓒ =

10. Order the following products from the least to the greatest

$\frac{3}{7}$ x 310, $1\frac{1}{2}$ x 310, $\frac{7}{7}$ x 310

Ⓐ $\frac{3}{7}$ x 310, $\frac{7}{7}$ x 310, $1\frac{1}{2}$ x 310

Ⓑ $1\frac{1}{2}$ x 310, $\frac{7}{7}$ x 310, $\frac{3}{7}$ x 310

Ⓒ $\frac{3}{7}$ x 310, $1\frac{1}{2}$ x 310, $\frac{7}{7}$ x 310

Ⓓ $1\frac{1}{2}$ x 310, $\frac{7}{7}$ x 310, $\frac{3}{7}$ x 310

Name _____   Date _____

Chapter 4

Lesson 8: Real World Problems with Fractions

You can scan the QR code given below or use the url to access additional EdSearch resources including videos and mobile apps related to *Real World Problems with Fractions*.

 **Real World Problems with Fractions**

URL	QR Code
http://www.lumoslearning.com/a/5nfb6	

1. Chef Chris is using $\frac{3}{4}$ lb. of chicken per person at a luncheon. If there are 17 people at the luncheon, how many pounds of chicken will he use?

    Ⓐ $12\frac{3}{4}$

    Ⓑ $\frac{51}{68}$

    Ⓒ $\frac{48}{4}$

    Ⓓ $17\frac{3}{4}$

2. A team of runners ran a relay race $\frac{9}{10}$ of a mile long. If Carl ran $\frac{3}{5}$ of the race, how far did his teammates run?

    Ⓐ $\frac{9}{25}$ mile

    Ⓑ $\frac{27}{50}$ mile

    Ⓒ $\frac{1}{10}$ mile

    Ⓓ $\frac{2}{5}$ mile

3. There are $1\frac{4}{5}$ pounds. of jelly beans in each bag. If Mrs. Lancer buys 3 bags of jelly beans for her class, how many pounds of jelly beans will she have in all?

    Ⓐ $3\frac{12}{15}$

    Ⓑ $5\frac{2}{5}$

    Ⓒ $3\frac{4}{15}$

    Ⓓ $5\frac{4}{5}$

4. Mario is in a bike race that is $3\frac{1}{5}$ miles long. He gets a flat tire $\frac{2}{3}$ of the way into the race. How many miles did he make it before he got a flat tire?

    Ⓐ $3\frac{2}{15}$

    Ⓑ $1\frac{3}{8}$

    Ⓒ $2\frac{2}{15}$

    Ⓓ $\frac{2}{3}$

5. Jackson is swimming laps in a pool that is $20\frac{1}{2}$ meters long. He swims $4\frac{1}{2}$ laps. How many meters did he swim?

Ⓐ $80\frac{1}{4}$

Ⓑ $92\frac{1}{4}$

Ⓒ $84\frac{1}{2}$

Ⓓ 90

6. A sack of potatoes weighs $4\frac{2}{3}$ lbs. If there are 20 sacks of potatoes in a crate, what is the total weight of the potatoes (in pounds)?

Ⓐ $93\frac{1}{3}$

Ⓑ $80\frac{40}{60}$

Ⓒ $80\frac{2}{3}$

Ⓓ $24\frac{2}{3}$

7. A factory packages bolts that are each $1\frac{1}{8}$ inches wide. If there are 6 bolts side-by-side in a package, how many inches wide must the packaging be?

Ⓐ $6\frac{1}{8}$

Ⓑ $7\frac{5}{8}$

Ⓒ $7\frac{1}{8}$

Ⓓ $6\frac{6}{8}$

8. There are 21 students in a fifth grade class. It takes their teacher $1\frac{1}{4}$ hours to complete each student's report card. How many hours will the report cards take all together?

Ⓐ $24\frac{3}{4}$

Ⓑ $21\frac{1}{4}$

Ⓒ $21\frac{21}{84}$

Ⓓ $26\frac{1}{4}$

9. Kara multiplied some measurements to determine that she needs $\frac{14}{3}$ yards of fabric for a project. How many yards of fabric should she ask for at the store?

Ⓐ $1\frac{4}{3}$

Ⓑ $14\frac{1}{3}$

Ⓒ $4\frac{2}{3}$

Ⓓ $2\frac{1}{3}$

10. Danny needs $5\frac{1}{4}$ feet of tile trim for his kitchen. The tile is sold in pieces that are $\frac{1}{4}$ of a foot long. How many pieces should he buy?

Ⓐ 6

Ⓑ 21

Ⓒ 20

Ⓓ $\frac{5}{16}$

11. Jacobi is making a ramp. If the area of the ramp must be less than 2 m² but more than 1 m² which of the following are possible dimensions of the ramp? Select all the correct answers.

Ⓐ Length = $1\frac{2}{5}$ m; Width = $1\frac{1}{6}$ m

Ⓑ Length = $2\frac{3}{4}$ m; Width = $\frac{7}{8}$ m

Ⓒ Length = $\frac{6}{5}$ m; Width = $\frac{8}{9}$ m

Ⓓ Length = $\frac{3}{7}$ m; Width = $2\frac{4}{5}$ m

12. Kendra ran 6 miles. Her friend Riley ran $\frac{2}{3}$ as far as Kendra. How far did Riley run? Simplify the answer and enter it in the box.

13. Leila is reading a book for school. On Monday she read $\frac{1}{12}$ of the book. On Tuesday she read $\frac{3}{4}$ as much as she read on Monday. What fraction of the book did Leila read on Tuesday? Circle the correct answer.

Ⓐ $\frac{5}{6}$

Ⓑ $\frac{1}{9}$

Ⓒ $\frac{1}{16}$

Ⓓ $\frac{3}{24}$

Chapter 4

Lesson 9: Dividing Fractions

You can scan the QR code given below or use the url to access additional EdSearch resources including videos and mobile apps related to *Dividing Fractions*.

Dividing Fractions

URL	QR Code
http://www.lumoslearning.com/a/5nfb7a	

1. **Divide: $2 \div \dfrac{1}{3} =$**

   Ⓐ 3
   Ⓑ 2
   Ⓒ 1
   Ⓓ 6

2. **In order to divide by a fraction you must first:**

   Ⓐ find its reciprocal
   Ⓑ match its denominator
   Ⓒ find its factors
   Ⓓ multiply by the numerator

3. **Divide: $3 \div \dfrac{2}{3} =$**

   Ⓐ $4\dfrac{2}{3}$
   Ⓑ $3\dfrac{2}{3}$
   Ⓒ 4
   Ⓓ $4\dfrac{1}{2}$

4. **Complete the following:**
   Dividing a number by a fraction less than 1 results in a quotient that is _____ the original number.

   Ⓐ the reciprocal of
   Ⓑ less than
   Ⓒ greater than
   Ⓓ equal to

5. **5 people want to evenly share a $\dfrac{1}{3}$ pound bag of peanuts. How many pounds should each person get?**

   Ⓐ $\dfrac{3}{5}$
   Ⓑ $1\dfrac{2}{3}$
   Ⓒ $\dfrac{3}{15}$
   Ⓓ $\dfrac{1}{15}$

6. A jeweler has $\dfrac{1}{8}$ of a pound of gold. If she uses it to make 4 bracelets, how many pounds of gold will be in each bracelet?

    Ⓐ $\dfrac{2}{16}$

    Ⓑ $\dfrac{1}{32}$

    Ⓒ $\dfrac{1}{4}$

    Ⓓ $\dfrac{4}{8}$

7. Tony is running a long distance race. If he stops for water every $\dfrac{1}{3}$ mile, how many times will he stop for water in a 10-mile race?

    Ⓐ 3.33
    Ⓑ 13
    Ⓒ 30
    Ⓓ 7

8. Which statement proves that $\dfrac{1}{6} \div 3 = \dfrac{1}{18}$?

    Ⓐ $\dfrac{3}{18} = \dfrac{1}{6}$

    Ⓑ $\dfrac{1}{6} \times 3 = \dfrac{3}{6}$

    Ⓒ $\dfrac{1}{18} \div 3 = \dfrac{1}{6}$

    Ⓓ $\dfrac{1}{18} \times 3 = \dfrac{3}{18}$

9. Dividing a fraction by a whole number makes it _____.

    Ⓐ smaller
    Ⓑ larger
    Ⓒ change to its reciprocal
    Ⓓ improper

10. The scout leader bought an 8-pound bag of trail mix. If he divides it into $\frac{1}{4}$ pound servings, how many servings will there be?

Ⓐ 20
Ⓑ 32
Ⓒ 4
Ⓓ 18

11. Which statement proves that $10 \div \frac{1}{4} = 40$?
Circle the correct answer

Ⓐ $\frac{1}{40} \times 10 = \frac{10}{40}$

Ⓑ $\frac{1}{4} \times \frac{1}{10} = \frac{1}{40}$

Ⓒ $40 \times \frac{1}{4} = 10$

Ⓓ $4 \times 10 = 40$

12. Read each equation below and mark whether the equation is true or false.

	True	False
$6 \div \frac{1}{3} > 16$	○	○
$\frac{1}{4} \div 3 = \frac{3}{12}$	○	○
$12 \div \frac{1}{6} < 80$	○	○
$\frac{1}{5} \div 2 > 9$	○	○

13. What four unit fractions complete the equations below? Enter your answers in the table.

2	÷		=	12
	÷	5	=	$\frac{1}{15}$
12	÷		=	48
	÷	4	=	$\frac{1}{28}$

LumosLearning.com

Chapter 4

Lesson 10: Dividing by Unit Fractions

You can scan the QR code given below or use the url to access additional EdSearch resources including videos and mobile apps related to *Dividing by Unit Fractions*.

Search **Dividing by Unit Fractions**

URL	QR Code
http://www.lumoslearning.com/a/5nfb7b	

1. Which best explains why $6 \div \dfrac{1}{4} = 24$?

   Ⓐ $24 \div \dfrac{1}{4} = 6$

   Ⓑ $24 \times \dfrac{1}{4} = 6$

   Ⓒ $24 \div 6 = \dfrac{1}{4}$

   Ⓓ $24 = \dfrac{1}{4} \times 6$

2. Which model best represents the following equation?
   $4 \div \dfrac{1}{3} = 12$

   Ⓐ

   Ⓑ

   Ⓒ

   Ⓓ

3. Which equation matches this model?

   Ⓐ $24 \div \dfrac{1}{8} = 3$

   Ⓑ $24 \div \dfrac{1}{3} = 8$

   Ⓒ $8 \div \dfrac{1}{3} = 24$

   Ⓓ $3 \div \dfrac{1}{8} = 24$

4. Byron has 5 pieces of wood from which to build his birdhouse. If he cuts each piece into fifths, how many pieces will he have?

Ⓐ 25
Ⓑ 5
Ⓒ $\frac{1}{5}$
Ⓓ $\frac{5}{25}$

5. Angelina has 10 yards of fabric. She needs $\frac{1}{3}$ yard of fabric for each purse she will sew. How many purses will she be able to make?

Ⓐ $3\frac{1}{3}$
Ⓑ $10\frac{1}{3}$
Ⓒ 30
Ⓓ 13

6. What is the value of 4 divided by $\frac{1}{5}$. Circle the correct answer choice.

Ⓐ $\frac{4}{5}$
Ⓑ 20
Ⓒ $\frac{1}{20}$
Ⓓ 9

7. Read each statement below and indicate whether it is true or false.

Statements	True	False
$\frac{1}{12} \div 4 > 40$	○	○
$\frac{1}{4} \div 7 = \frac{1}{14}$	○	○
$\frac{1}{3} \div 33 < 5$	○	○
$\frac{1}{8} \div 4 < \frac{1}{2}$	○	○

8. **What three unit fractions complete the equations below? Enter your answers into the table.**

	÷	14	=	$\frac{1}{112}$
	÷	29	=	$\frac{1}{87}$
	÷	55	=	$\frac{1}{495}$

9. **Evaluate** $8 \div \frac{1}{3}$.

   Ⓐ 24
   Ⓑ 27
   Ⓒ 21
   Ⓓ 2.7

10. **Evaluate** $4 \div \frac{7}{21}$.

   Ⓐ 7
   Ⓑ 12
   Ⓒ 27
   Ⓓ 36

Chapter 4

Lesson 11: Real World Problems Dividing Fractions

You can scan the QR code given below or use the url to access additional EdSearch resources including videos and mobile apps related to *Real World Problems* Dividing Fractions.

 **Real World Problems Dividing Fractions**

URL	QR Code
http://www.lumoslearning.com/a/5nfb7c	

1. Darren has a 3 cup bag of snack mix. Each serving is $\frac{1}{4}$ cup. Which model will help him determine how many $\frac{1}{4}$ cup servings are in the whole bag of snack mix?

   Ⓐ

   Ⓑ

   Ⓒ

   Ⓓ

2. Which situation could be represented by the following model?

   Ⓐ The number of $\frac{1}{8}$ lb. servings of cheese in 4 lbs. of cheese
   Ⓑ Four friends share 8 lbs. of cheese
   Ⓒ 4 lbs. of cheese divided into 8 equal servings
   Ⓓ The amount of cheese needed for 8 people to each have $\frac{1}{4}$ lb.

3. A team of 3 runners competes in a $\frac{1}{4}$ mile relay race. If each person runs an equal portion of the race, how far does each person run?

   Ⓐ $\frac{3}{7}$ mile
   Ⓑ $\frac{3}{12}$ mile
   Ⓒ $\frac{3}{4}$ mile
   Ⓓ $\frac{1}{12}$ mile

4. A beaker holds $\frac{1}{10}$ of a liter of water. If the water is divided equally into 6 test tubes, how much water will be in each test tube?

Ⓐ $\frac{1}{60}$ liter

Ⓑ $\frac{6}{10}$ liter

Ⓒ $\frac{1}{6}$ liter

Ⓓ $\frac{10}{16}$ liter

5. Mrs. Blake orders 3 pizzas for a school party. If each slice is $\frac{1}{12}$ of a pizza, how many slices are there in all?

Ⓐ 24

Ⓑ $4\frac{1}{3}$

Ⓒ 36

Ⓓ $\frac{3}{12}$

6. Lawson, Rhett and Wynn bought packages of silly putty. Lawson divided each of his five packages into thirds, Rhett divided each of his four packages into fourths and Wynn divided each of his 3 packages into fifths. Based on this information, which of the following two statements are true.

Ⓐ Lawson and Wynn have the same number of portions of silly putty.
Ⓑ Wynn has five more portions of silly putty than Rhett.
Ⓒ Rhett has more portions of silly putty than Lawson.
Ⓓ Lawson, Rhett and Wynn all have the same number of portions of silly putty.

7. Mrs. Klein has a small rectangular area in her backyard to use for composting. If the width of the rectangular area is $1\frac{1}{7}$ yards and the compost area must be less than 6 square yards, what is the maximum length of the garden?
Enter your answer in the box below.

8. The basketball coach advised all players to drink 2500 milliliters of water during the day before each game. How much is this in liters?

   Ⓐ 0.25 liters
   Ⓑ 2.5 liters
   Ⓒ 25 liters
   Ⓓ 250 liters

9. Sam is painting his house. If he needs $\frac{1}{2}$ liter of paint per room. How many liters of paint is required to paint 4 rooms?

   Ⓐ 2 liters
   Ⓑ 3 liters
   Ⓒ 4 liters
   Ⓓ 5 liters

10. Mathew has $\frac{4}{5}$ of a tank of fuel in his car. He needs 1/10 of a tank per day. How many days will the fuel in his tank last?

   Ⓐ 6 days
   Ⓑ 8 days
   Ⓒ 5 days
   Ⓓ 7 days

End of Numbers and Operations – Fractions

Chapter 5: Measurement and Data

Lesson 1: Converting Units of Measure

You can scan the QR code given below or use the url to access additional EdSearch resources including videos and mobile apps related to *Converting Units of Measure*.

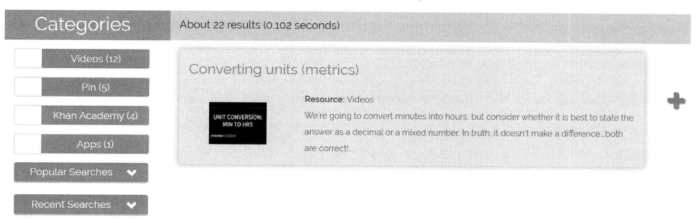

Categories   About 22 results (0.102 seconds)

Videos (12)

Pin (5)   Converting units (metrics)

Khan Academy (4)   **Resource:** Videos

Apps (1)   We're going to convert minutes into hours, but consider whether it is best to state the answer as a decimal or a mixed number. In truth, it doesn't make a difference...both are correct!...

Popular Searches ∨

Recent Searches ∨

ed)Search *Converting Units of Measure*

URL	QR Code
http://www.lumoslearning.com/a/5mda1	

1. **Complete the following.**
    1 inch equals the same length as _____ centimeters.

    Ⓐ 0.6
    Ⓑ 2.54
    Ⓒ 10
    Ⓓ 2.0

2. **Complete the following.**
    10 cm = 1 ___

    Ⓐ km
    Ⓑ dm
    Ⓒ mm
    Ⓓ m

3. **Keith has 7 yards of string. How many inches of string does he have?**

    Ⓐ 112 inches
    Ⓑ 224 inches
    Ⓒ 84 inches
    Ⓓ 252 inches

4. **Which of these is the most reasonable estimate for the total area of the floor space in a house?**

    Ⓐ 1,200 sq km
    Ⓑ 1,200 sq in
    Ⓒ 120 sq in
    Ⓓ 1,200 sq ft

5. **Complete the following.**
    2.25 hours = _____ minutes

    Ⓐ 135
    Ⓑ 225
    Ⓒ 145
    Ⓓ 150

6. The normal body temperature of a person in degrees Celsius is about _____.

   Ⓐ 0 degrees Celsius
   Ⓑ 37 degrees Celsius
   Ⓒ 95 degrees Celsius
   Ⓓ 12 degrees Celsius

7. There are 8 pints in a gallon. How many times greater is the volume of a gallon compared to a pint?

   Ⓐ 8 times greater
   Ⓑ $\frac{1}{8}$ times greater
   Ⓒ twice as great
   Ⓓ $\frac{8}{10}$ as great

8. Which of the following measures about 1 dm in length?

   Ⓐ a car
   Ⓑ a new crayon
   Ⓒ a ladybug
   Ⓓ a football field

9. Complete the following.
   The area of a postage stamp is about _____ .

   Ⓐ 100 sq in
   Ⓑ 4 sq in
   Ⓒ 10 sq in
   Ⓓ 1 sq in

10. Complete the following.
    A fully loaded moving truck might weigh _____ .

    Ⓐ 5 tons
    Ⓑ 50 tons
    Ⓒ 500 ounces
    Ⓓ 5,000 ounces

11. **Read the conversions and indicate whether they are true or false.**

	True	False
45 quarts = 90 cups	○	○
15 liters = 15,000 milliliters	○	○
5 pounds = 80 ounces	○	○
60 inches = 5 feet	○	○

12. **A meter is 100 centimeters. If a track is 500 meters long. How long is the track in centimeters? Enter your answer in the box given below.**

13. **Complete the following statement:**
75 nickels has the same value as _____ quarters.

14. **Kale made 5 gallons of sports drink for the baseball team. Which of the following represents the same quantity? Select all the correct answers.**

Ⓐ 20 quarts
Ⓑ 32 pints
Ⓒ 40 cups
Ⓓ 640 ounces

Name _____   Date _____

Chapter 5

Lesson 2: Representing and Interpreting Data

You can scan the QR code given below or use the url to access additional EdSearch resources including videos and mobile apps related to *Representing and Interpreting Data*.

Representing and Interpreting Data

URL	QR Code
http://www.lumoslearning.com/a/5mdb2	

1. **A 5th grade science class is raising mealworms. The students measured the mealworms and recorded the lengths on this line plot.**

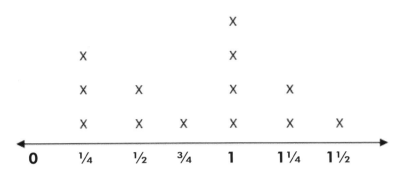

Length of Mealworms

Inches

According to this line plot, what was the length of the longest mealworm?

Ⓐ $\frac{1}{4}$ inch

Ⓑ $\frac{3}{4}$ inch

Ⓒ 1 inch

Ⓓ $1\frac{1}{2}$ inches

2. **A 5th grade science class is raising mealworms. The students measured the mealworms and recorded the lengths on this line plot.**

Length of Mealworms

```
                        X
        X               X
        X    X          X    X
        X    X    X     X    X    X
   ◄────┼────┼────┼─────┼────┼────┼──────►
   0   ¼    ½    ¾    1   1¼   1½
```

Inches

According to this line plot, what was the length of the shortest mealworm?

Ⓐ $\frac{1}{4}$ inch

Ⓑ $\frac{3}{4}$ inch

Ⓒ $1\frac{1}{4}$ inch

Ⓓ 0

3. A 5th grade science class is raising mealworms. The students measured the mealworms and recorded the lengths on this line plot.

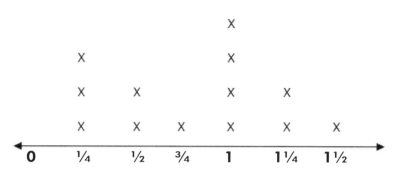

Length of Mealworms

Inches

According to this line plot, what was the most common length for mealworms?

Ⓐ $1\frac{1}{2}$ inches

Ⓑ $\frac{3}{4}$ inch

Ⓒ $\frac{1}{4}$ inch

Ⓓ 1 inch

4. A 5th grade science class is raising mealworms. The students measured the mealworms and recorded the lengths on this line plot.

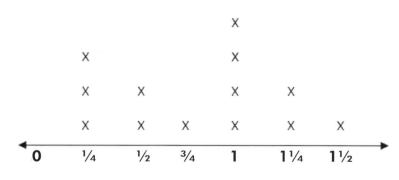

Length of Mealworms

Inches

According to this line plot, how many mealworms were less than 1 inch long?

Ⓐ 4

Ⓑ 6

Ⓒ 3

Ⓓ 2

5. **A 5th grade science class is raising mealworms. The students measured the mealworms and recorded the lengths on this line plot.**

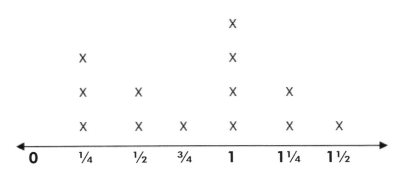

Length of Mealworms

```
                              X
              X               X
              X       X       X       X
              X       X   X   X   X   X
    ◄─────────────────────────────────────────►
        0    ¼     ½    ¾    1    1¼   1½
```

Inches

According to this line plot, how many mealworms were measured in all?

Ⓐ 4
Ⓑ 10
Ⓒ 13
Ⓓ 27 $\frac{3}{4}$

6. **A 5th grade science class is raising mealworms. The students measured the mealworms and recorded the lengths on this line plot.**

Length of Mealworms

```
                              X
              X               X
              X       X       X       X
              X       X   X   X   X   X
    ◄─────────────────────────────────────────►
        0    ¼     ½    ¾    1    1¼   1½
```

Inches

According to this line plot, what is the median length of a mealworm?

Ⓐ 1 inch
Ⓑ 13 inches
Ⓒ between $\frac{3}{4}$ inch and 1 inch
Ⓓ 1$\frac{1}{2}$ inches

7. A 5th grade science class is raising mealworms. The students measured the mealworms and recorded the lengths on this line plot.

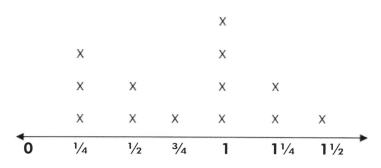

Length of Mealworms

Inches

How could someone use this line plot to find the total length of all the mealworms?

Ⓐ Add each of the numbers along the bottom of the line plot
Ⓑ Multiply each of the numbers along the bottom of the line plot
Ⓒ Multiply each length by its number of Xs, then add the values
Ⓓ Multiply each of the numbers along the bottom of the line plot by the total number of Xs, then add the values

8. A 5th grade science class is raising mealworms. The students measured the mealworms and recorded the lengths on this line plot.

Length of Mealworms

| 0 | ¼ | ½ | ¾ | 1 | 1¼ | 1½ |

Inches

Which of these mealworm lengths would not fit within the range of this line plot?

Ⓐ $\frac{7}{8}$ inch

Ⓑ $1\frac{3}{4}$ inches

Ⓒ $1\frac{1}{8}$ inches

Ⓓ $\frac{5}{16}$ inch

9. A 5th grade science class is observing weather conditions. The students measured the amount of precipitation each day and recorded it on this line plot.

Days of Precipitation

```
            X
            X
            X           X
            X    X    X              X
    X       X    X    X    X         X
  ◄─────────────────────────────────────────────►
    0   1/10  2/10 3/10 4/10 5/10 6/10 7/10 8/10 9/10  1
                          mL
```

According to this line plot, what was the most precipitation recorded in one day?

Ⓐ $4\frac{7}{10}$ mL

Ⓑ $\frac{7}{10}$ mL

Ⓒ $\frac{9}{10}$ mL

Ⓓ $\frac{2}{10}$ mL

10. A 5th grade science class is observing weather conditions. The students measured the amount of precipitation each day and recorded it on this line plot.

Days of Precipitation

```
            X
            X
            X           X
            X    X    X              X
    X       X    X    X    X         X
  ◄─────────────────────────────────────────────►
    0   1/10  2/10 3/10 4/10 5/10 6/10 7/10 8/10 9/10  1
                          mL
```

According to this line plot, what was the least amount of precipitation that fell on days that had precipitation?

Ⓐ $\frac{1}{10}$ mL

Ⓑ $\frac{6}{10}$ mL

Ⓒ 0 mL

Ⓓ $\frac{2}{10}$ mL

11. A 5th grade science class is observing weather conditions. The students measured the amount of precipitation each day and recorded it on this line plot.

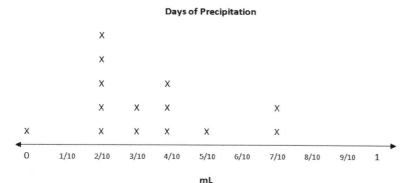

According to this line plot, what was the most common amount of precipitation?

Ⓐ $\frac{7}{10}$ mL

Ⓑ $\frac{9}{10}$ mL

Ⓒ $\frac{2}{10}$ mL

Ⓓ 0 mL

12. A 5th grade science class is observing weather conditions. The students measured the amount of precipitation each day and recorded it on this line plot.

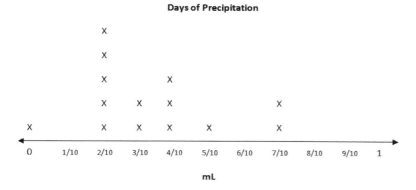

According to this line plot, how many days received less than $\frac{3}{10}$ mL of precipitation?

Ⓐ 6

Ⓑ 0

Ⓒ 4

Ⓓ 3

13. A 5th grade science class is observing weather conditions. The students measured the amount of precipitation each day and recorded it on this line plot.

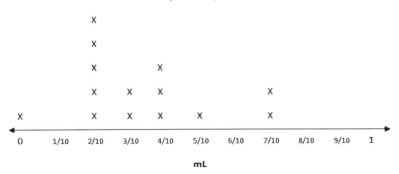

According to this line plot, how many days were observed in all?

Ⓐ 13
Ⓑ 5
Ⓒ 14
Ⓓ 11

14. A 5th grade science class is observing weather conditions. The students measured the amount of precipitation each day and recorded it on this line plot.

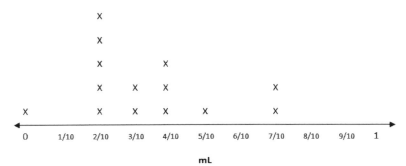

According to this line plot, what is the median amount of precipitation?

Ⓐ $\frac{7}{10}$ mL

Ⓑ $\frac{3}{10}$ mL

Ⓒ $\frac{2}{10}$ mL

Ⓓ 0 mL

15. A 5th grade science class is observing weather conditions. The students measured the amount of precipitation each day and recorded it on this line plot.

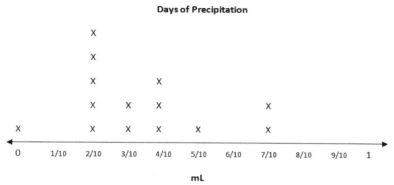

How could someone use this line plot to find the total amount of all the precipitation that fell?

Ⓐ Add each of the numbers along the bottom of the line plot
Ⓑ Multiply each of the numbers along the bottom of the line plot by the total number of Xs, then add the values
Ⓒ Multiply each of the numbers along the bottom of the line plot
Ⓓ Multiply each measurement by its number of Xs, then add the values

16. A 5th grade science class is observing weather conditions. The students measured the amount of precipitation each day and recorded it on this line plot.

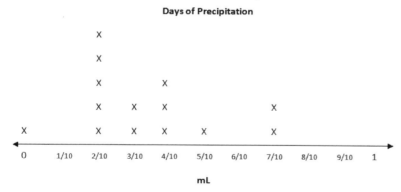

Which of these measurements would not fit within the range of this line plot?

Ⓐ $\frac{12}{10}$ mL
Ⓑ $\frac{9}{10}$ mL
Ⓒ 0 mL
Ⓓ $\frac{2}{10}$ mL

17. A 5th grade science class is observing weather conditions. The students measured the amount of precipitation each day and recorded it on this line plot.

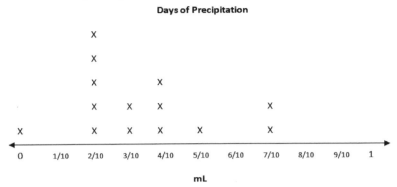

Suppose the class recorded data for one more day, but there was no precipitation. What should they do?

Ⓐ Leave the line plot as it is
Ⓑ Add an X above the one in the 0 column
Ⓒ Erase one of the Xs from the line plot
Ⓓ Make up a value and put an X in that column

18. A 5th grade science class went on a nature walk. Each of the students selected one leaf and weighed it when they got back to the room. They recorded their data on this line plot.

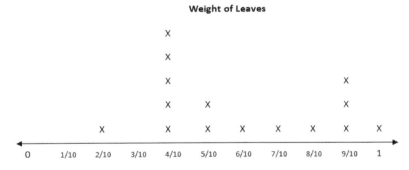

According to this line plot, which is the least frequent weight of a leaf?

Ⓐ $\frac{7}{10}$ g
Ⓑ $\frac{9}{10}$ g
Ⓒ $\frac{4}{10}$ g
Ⓓ $\frac{5}{10}$ g

LumosLearning.com

19. A 5th grade science class went on a nature walk. Each of the students selected one leaf and weighed it when they got back to the room. They recorded their data on this line plot.

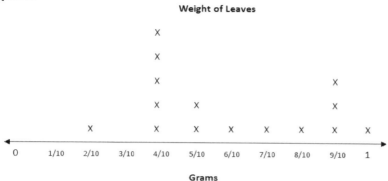

According to this line plot, what is the range of weights for these leaves?

Ⓐ $\frac{8}{10}$ g

Ⓑ 1 g

Ⓒ $\frac{5}{10}$ g

Ⓓ $\frac{4}{10}$ g

20. A 5th grade science class went on a nature walk. Each of the students selected one leaf and weighed it when they got back to the room. They recorded their data on this line plot.

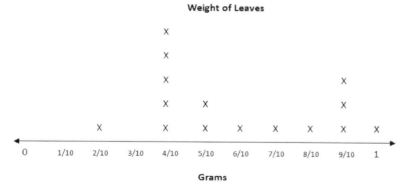

According to this line plot, what is the mode for this set of data?

Ⓐ 1

Ⓑ 15

Ⓒ $\frac{5}{10}$

Ⓓ $\frac{4}{10}$

21. A 5th grade science class went on a nature walk. Each of the students selected one leaf and weighed it when they got back to the room. They recorded their data on this line plot.

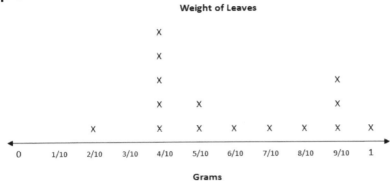

According to this line plot, how many leaves weigh more than $\frac{7}{10}$ g?

Ⓐ 1
Ⓑ 5
Ⓒ 9
Ⓓ 0

22. A 5th grade science class went on a nature walk. Each of the students selected one leaf and weighed it when they got back to the room. They recorded their data on this line plot.

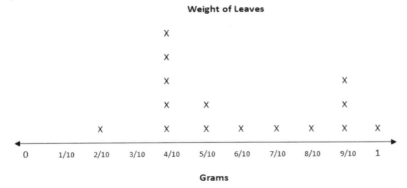

According to this line plot, how many leaves were measured in all?

Ⓐ 15
Ⓑ $\frac{4}{10}$
Ⓒ $\frac{6}{10}$
Ⓓ 11

23. A 5th grade science class went on a nature walk. Each of the students selected one leaf and weighed it when they got back to the room. They recorded their data on this line plot.

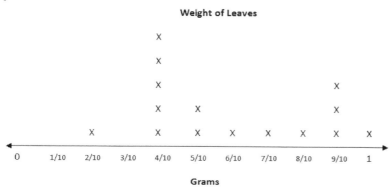

According to this line plot, how many leaves weigh less than the most frequent weight?

Ⓐ 9
Ⓑ 5
Ⓒ 0
Ⓓ 1

24. A 5th grade science class went on a nature walk. Each of the students selected one leaf and weighed it when they got back to the room. They recorded their data on this line plot.

What is the total weight of all the leaves?

Ⓐ 9 g
Ⓑ $\frac{9}{10}$ g
Ⓒ 90 g
Ⓓ $\frac{9}{100}$ g

25. A 5th grade science class went on a nature walk. Each of the students selected one leaf and weighed it when they got back to the room. They recorded their data on this line plot.

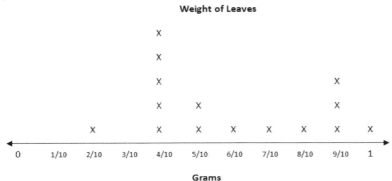

Weight of Leaves

Grams

What is the average weight of the leaves?

Ⓐ $\frac{5}{10}$ g

Ⓑ $\frac{9}{10}$ g

Ⓒ $\frac{6}{10}$ g

Ⓓ $\frac{8}{10}$ g

26. The line plot below shows the weight in fractions of a gram for fifteen pieces of mail. How much does each of the 3 pieces of mails next to 1/2 gram weigh?

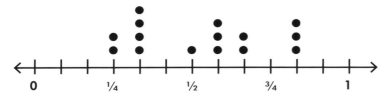

LumosLearning.com

27. The line plot below shows the length in fractions of an inch of several pieces of tile all having the same width. If the pieces were lined up length to length, how long would the line of tiles be? Circle the correct answer.

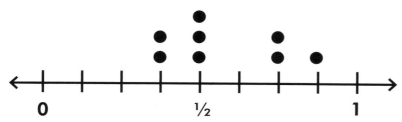

Ⓐ $3\dfrac{1}{4}$

Ⓑ $3\dfrac{5}{8}$

Ⓒ $1\dfrac{4}{8}$

Ⓓ $4\dfrac{5}{8}$

28. Tabitha made a line plot of the following data

$$\frac{1}{6}, \frac{2}{3}, \frac{1}{2}, \frac{1}{6}, \frac{5}{6}, \frac{4}{6}, \frac{6}{6}, \frac{3}{6}, \frac{1}{6}$$

Circle the line plot that represents this data.

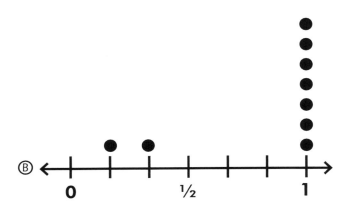

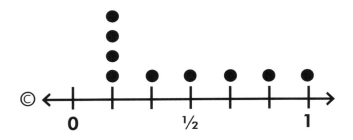

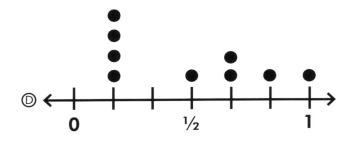

LumosLearning.com

Name _____   **Date** _____

Chapter 5

You can scan the QR code given below or use the url to access additional EdSearch resources including videos and mobile apps related to *Volume*.

 **ed Search**   ***Volume***

URL	QR Code
http://www.lumoslearning.com/a/5mdc3a	

1. **Which type of unit might be used to record the volume of a rectangular prism?**

    Ⓐ inches
    Ⓑ square inches
    Ⓒ ounces
    Ⓓ cubic inches

2. **Maeve needed to pack a crate that measured 4 ft. by 2 ft. by 3 ft. with 1 foot cubes. How many 1 foot cubes can she fit in the crate?**

    Ⓐ 12
    Ⓑ 48
    Ⓒ 24
    Ⓓ 9

3. **The volume of an object is the amount of _____.**

    Ⓐ space it occupies
    Ⓑ dimensions it has
    Ⓒ layers you can put in it
    Ⓓ weight it can hold

4. **Which of these could be filled with about 160 cubes of sugar if each sugar cube is one cubic centimeter?**

    Ⓐ a ring box
    Ⓑ a moving box
    Ⓒ a cereal box
    Ⓓ a sandbox

5. **Tony and Yolani are measuring the volume of a supply box at school. Tony uses a ruler to measure the box's length, width, and height in centimeters; then he multiplies these measurements. Yolani fills the box with centimeter cubes, then counts the number of cubes. How will their answers compare?**

    Ⓐ They cannot be compared because they used different units.
    Ⓑ They will be almost or exactly the same.
    Ⓒ Tony's answer will be greater than Yolani's.
    Ⓓ Yolani's answer will be greater than Tony's.

6. **Complete the following:**
   A cereal box has a volume of about _____ .

   (A) 3.0 cubic inches
   (B) 3,000 cubic inches
   (C) 30 cubic inches
   (D) 300 cubic inches

7. **Complete the following:**
   The correct formula for finding the volume of a rectangular box with length l, width w, and height h is _____.

   (A) $V = l \times w \times h$
   (B) $V = l \times w + h$
   (C) $V = w \times h + l$
   (D) $V = l + w + h$

8. **What is the volume of a box that measures 36 in. by 24 in. by 24 in.?**

   (A) 20,763 cubic inches
   (B) 84 cubic inches
   (C) 20,736 cubic inches
   (D) 111 cubic inches

9. **What is the volume of a box that measures 8 by 3 by 12 inches?**

   (A) 882 cubic inches
   (B) 23 cubic inches
   (C) 280 cubic inches
   (D) 288 cubic inches

10. **What is the volume of a cube that measures 3 by 3 by 3 centimeters?**

    (A) 9 cubic cm
    (B) 12 cubic cm
    (C) 27 cubic cm
    (D) 6 cubic cm

11. Which of the following cubes is a unit cube? Select Yes or No.

	YES	NO
3 cm / 4 cm / 1 cm	○	○
1 in / 1 in / 1 in	○	○
6 m / 6 m / 6 m	○	○
1 unit / 1 unit	○	○

12. Oscar wants to determine the volume of the chest, shown in the picture, in cubic inches. Complete the sentence below describing the dimensions of the unit cube.

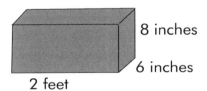

8 inches

6 inches

2 feet

Unit cube length	
Unit cube width	
Unit cube height	

13. Isaiah needs to determine the volume of his locker as shown in the picture. Which of the following unit cubes can he use to find the volume? Select the two correct answers.

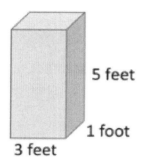

5 feet

1 foot

3 feet

Ⓐ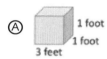

1 foot
1 foot
3 feet

Ⓑ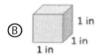

1 in
1 in
1 in

Ⓒ

5 feet
1 foot
3 feet

Ⓓ

1 foot
1 foot
1 foot

Chapter 5

Lesson 4: Cubic Units

You can scan the QR code given below or use the url to access additional EdSearch resources including videos and mobile apps related to *Cubic Units*.

ed)Search   *Cubic Units*

URL	QR Code
http://www.lumoslearning.com/a/5mdc3b	

1. Stan covers the bottom of a box with 8 centimeter cubes, leaving no gaps. He is able to build 4 layers of cubes to fill the box completely. What is the volume of the box?

    Ⓐ 256 centimeters
    Ⓑ The square of 256 cm
    Ⓒ 256 cm^2
    Ⓓ 256 cubic centimeters

2. Which of these is an accurate way to measure the volume of a rectangular prism?

    Ⓐ Fill it with water and then weigh the water
    Ⓑ Trace each face of the prism on centimeter grid paper, and then count the number of squares it comprises
    Ⓒ Measure the length and the width, and then multiply the two values
    Ⓓ Pack it with unit cubes, leaving no gaps or overlaps, and count the number of unit cubes

3. Which of these could possibly be the volume of a cereal box?

    Ⓐ 360 in^3
    Ⓑ 520 sq cm
    Ⓒ 400 cubic feet
    Ⓓ 385 dm^2

4. A container measures 4 inches wide, 6 inches long, and 10 inches high. How many 1 inch cubes will it hold?

    Ⓐ 20^2
    Ⓑ 240
    Ⓒ The cube of 240
    Ⓓ Cannot be determined

5. Annie covers the bottom of a box with 6 centimeter cubes (A centimeter cube is a cube of dimensions 1 cm x 1 cm x 1 cm), leaving no gaps. If the volume of the box is 30 cm^3, how many more centimeter cubes will she be able to fit inside?

    Ⓐ 5
    Ⓑ 180
    Ⓒ 24
    Ⓓ 4

6. The rectangular prism shown has 4 layers and each layer has 12 cubes. If one cube is equal to 1 cubic centimeter, what is the volume of the prism? Enter your answer in the box given below.

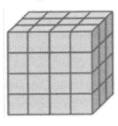 **Key:** ☐ represents one cubic unit

```
┌─────────────────────────────────────────────┐
│                                               │
│                                               │
│                                               │
│                                               │
└─────────────────────────────────────────────┘
```

7. What is the volume of the rectangular prism? Circle the correct answer choice.

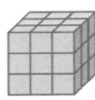 **Key:** ☐ represents one cubic unit

Ⓐ 27 cubic units
Ⓑ 18 cubic units
Ⓒ 16 cubic units
Ⓓ 21 cubic units

8. Select the picture that has a volume of 12 cubic units.
   Key: ☐ represents one cubic unit

Ⓐ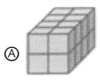

Ⓑ

Ⓒ

Ⓓ

9. What is the volume of this figure?

Key: ☐ **represents one cubic unit**

Ⓐ 12
Ⓑ 16
Ⓒ 18
Ⓓ 20

10. What is the volume of this figure?

Key: ☐ **represents one cubic unit**

Ⓐ 6
Ⓑ 8
Ⓒ 9
Ⓓ 10

Chapter 5

Lesson 5: Counting Cubic Units

You can scan the QR code given below or use the url to access additional EdSearch resources including videos and mobile apps related to *Counting Cubic Units*.

 **Counting Cubic Units**

URL	QR Code
http://www.lumoslearning.com/a/5mdc4	

1. **What is the volume of the figure?**

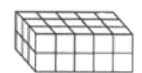

    Ⓐ 60 cubic units
    Ⓑ 15 cubic units
    Ⓒ 30 cubic units
    Ⓓ 31 cubic units

2. **What is the volume of the figure?**

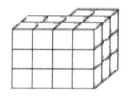

    Ⓐ 30 units^3
    Ⓑ 27 units^3
    Ⓒ 31 units^3
    Ⓓ 36 units^3

3. **Which of these has a volume of 24 cubic units?**

Ⓐ

Ⓑ

Ⓒ

Ⓓ

4. Trevor is building a tower out of centimeter cubes. This is the base of the tower so far.

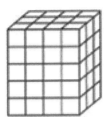

How many more layers must Trevor add to have a tower with a volume of 84 cm³?

Ⓐ 7
Ⓑ 2
Ⓒ 5
Ⓓ 4

5. Kerry built the figure on the left and Milo built the one on the right. If they knock down their two figures to build one large one using all of the blocks, what will its volume be?

Ⓐ 34 cubic units
Ⓑ 16 cubic units
Ⓒ 52 cubic units
Ⓓ 40 cubic units

6. Garrett must build a building that has a volume of 11 cubic meters. Look at the buildings below and indicate which are possible designs for his building.
Volume of one cube is one cubic meter.

	Yes	No
	◯	◯
	◯	◯
	◯	◯
	◯	◯

7. Use the picture of the solid below to complete the table. Write the numbers (only) in the blank spaces provided.

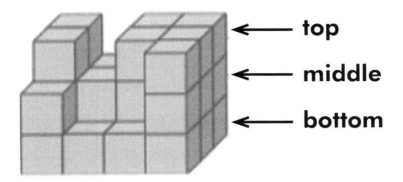

Number of cubes in the bottom layer	
Number of cubes in the middle layer	
Number of cubes in the top layer	
Volume of the solid	

Chapter 5

Lesson 6: Multiply to Find Volume

You can scan the QR code given below or use the url to access additional EdSearch resources including videos and mobile apps related to *Multiply to Find Volume*.

 Multiply to Find Volume

URL	QR Code
http://www.lumoslearning.com/a/5mdc5a	

1. **What is the volume of the figure?**

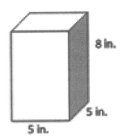

8 in.
5 in.
5 in.

Ⓐ 33 in³
Ⓑ 18 in³
Ⓒ 80 in³
Ⓓ 200 in³

2. **What is the volume of the figure?**

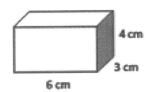

4 cm
3 cm
6 cm

Ⓐ 13 cm³
Ⓑ 22 cm³
Ⓒ 72 cm³
Ⓓ 700 cm³

3. **The figure has a volume of 66 ft³. What is the height of the figure?**

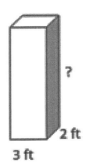

?
2 ft
3 ft

Ⓐ 11 ft
Ⓑ 61 ft
Ⓒ 13 ft
Ⓓ 33 ft

4. The figure has a volume of 14 in³. What is the width of the figure?

Ⓐ 2 inches
Ⓑ 1 inch
Ⓒ 5 inches
Ⓓ 2.5 inches

5. Which figure has a volume of 42 m³?

Ⓐ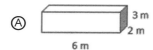

Ⓑ

Ⓒ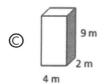

Ⓓ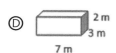

6. Use the picture to answer the question.

Which of the following will result in the volume of the figure. Note that more than one option may be correct.

Ⓐ 3 X 4 X 2
Ⓑ (4 X 3) + 2
Ⓒ 8 X 3
Ⓓ 12 + 2

7. Piko filled a box with 4 layers of cubes that measured one foot on each side. If the bottom of the box fits 6 cubes, What is the volume of the box? Enter the answer in the box.

8. Sarah is making a rectangular prism with base as shown below.

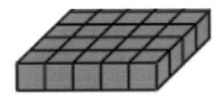

She plans to have a height of 5 cubes. Find the volume of the rectangular prism.

Ⓐ 110 cubic units
Ⓑ 100 cubic units
Ⓒ 125 cubic units
Ⓓ 135 cubic units

9. If the base of rectangular prism is as shown below and has a height of 4 units, what will be the volume of the prism?

Ⓐ 32 cubic units
Ⓑ 36 cubic units
Ⓒ 48 cubic units
Ⓓ 54 cubic units

10. The base of a rectangular prism has an area of 25 square units. The height of the rectangular prism is 2 units. What is the volume of the prism?

Ⓐ 50 cubic units
Ⓑ 100 cubic units
Ⓒ 75 cubic units
Ⓓ 125 cubic units

Name _____   **Date** _____

Chapter 5

Lesson 7: Real World Problems with Volume

You can scan the QR code given below or use the url to access additional EdSearch resources including videos and mobile apps related to *Real World Problems with Volume*.

 Real World Problems with Volume

URL	QR Code
http://www.lumoslearning.com/a/5mdc5b	

1. Michael packed a box full of 1 ft cubes. The box held 54 cubes. Which of these could be the box Michael packed?

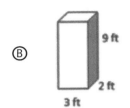

Ⓐ   6 ft, 2 ft, 3 ft

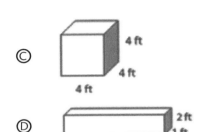

Ⓑ   9 ft, 2 ft, 3 ft

Ⓒ   4 ft, 4 ft, 4 ft

Ⓓ   18 ft, 2 ft, 1 ft

2. A container is shaped like a rectangular prism. The area of its base is 30 in². If the container is 5 inches tall, how many 1 inch cubes can it hold?

Ⓐ 150
Ⓑ 35
Ⓒ 4500
Ⓓ 95

3. A rectangular prism has a volume of 300 cm³. If the area of its base is 25 cm² how tall is the prism?

Ⓐ 325 cm
Ⓑ 7500 cm
Ⓒ 12 cm
Ⓓ 275 cm

4. Antonia wants to buy a jewelry box with the greatest volume. She measures the length, width, and height of four different jewelry boxes. Which one should she buy to have the greatest volume?

Ⓐ 10 in x 7 in x 4 in
Ⓑ 8 in x 5 in x 5 in
Ⓒ 12 in x 5 in x 5 in
Ⓓ 14 in x 2 in x 10 in

LumosLearning.com

5. Damien is building a file cabinet that must hold 20 ft³. He has created a base for the cabinet that is 4 ft by 1 ft. How tall should he build the cabinet?

Ⓐ 25 ft
Ⓑ 20 ft
Ⓒ 4 ft
Ⓓ 5 ft

6. Bethany has a small rectangular garden that is 32 inches long by 14 inches wide. The average depth of the soil is 2 inches. If Bethany wanted to replace the soil, how much would she need? Circle the correct answer choice.

Ⓐ 448 in³
Ⓑ 896 in³
Ⓒ 450 in³
Ⓓ 48 in³

7. A building has a volume of 1520 ft³. The area of the base of the building is 95 ft². What is the height of the building?

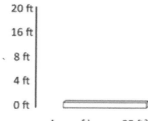

20 ft
16 ft
8 ft
4 ft
0 ft

Area of base = 95 ft²

Ⓐ 20ft
Ⓑ 16ft
Ⓒ 8ft
Ⓓ 4ft

8. Melanie has a jewelry box with the volume of 36 cubic cms. If the width is 4 cms and the height is 3 cms, then what is the length of the box?

Ⓐ 4 cms
Ⓑ 3 cms
Ⓒ 5 cms
Ⓓ 12 cms

9. Henry is building an aquarium. The length of the aquarium is 4 feet, width is 3 feet and the height is 5 feet. What will be the volume of the aquarium?

Ⓐ 64 cubic feet
Ⓑ 72 cubic feet
Ⓒ 60 cubic feet
Ⓓ 81 cubic feet.

10. Volume of a clothes box is 2m x 1m x 2m. 15 such boxes must be loaded in a tanker. What will be the total volume occupied by the boxes?

Ⓐ 72 cubic meters
Ⓑ 64 cubic meters
Ⓒ 81 cubic meters
Ⓓ 60 cubic meters

LumosLearning.com

Name _____ **Date** _____

Chapter 5

You can scan the QR code given below or use the url to access additional EdSearch resources including videos and mobile apps related to *Adding Volumes*.

 **Adding Volumes**

URL	QR Code
http://www.lumoslearning.com/a/5mdc5c	

1. A refrigerator has a 3 foot by 2 foot base. The refrigerator portion is 4 feet high and the freezer is 2 feet high. What is the total volume?

    Ⓐ 36 ft³
    Ⓑ 26 ft³
    Ⓒ 11 ft³
    Ⓓ 16 ft³

2. Matthew has two identical coolers. Each one measures 30 inches long, 10 inches wide, and 15 inches high. What is the total volume of the two coolers?

    Ⓐ 4,500 in³
    Ⓑ 9,000 in³
    Ⓒ 110 in³
    Ⓓ 3,025 in³

3. Ingrid is packing 1 foot square boxes into shipping crates. She has two shipping crates, shown below. How many boxes can she pack in them all together?

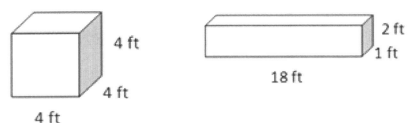

    Ⓐ 64
    Ⓑ 33
    Ⓒ 82
    Ⓓ 100

4. Bryson has two identical bookcases stacked one on top of the other. Together, they hold 48 ft³. If the area of the base is 8 ft², how tall is each bookcase?

    Ⓐ 40 ft
    Ⓑ 6 ft
    Ⓒ 3 ft
    Ⓓ 20 ft

5. Amy built a house for her gerbil out of two boxes. One box measures 6 cm by 3 cm by 10 cm and the other measures 4 cm by 2 cm by 2 cm. What is the total volume of the gerbil house?

Ⓐ 196 cm³
Ⓑ 180 cm³
Ⓒ 27 cm³
Ⓓ 2,880 cm³

6. Jade and her brother Seth are going on a hiking trip. Together they can bring a total of 345 in³ of supplies. Indicate by checking yes or no the possible dimensions of the box each can bring.

	Yes	No
Jade: 4 in X 12 in X4 in Seth: 8 in X 7 in X 3 in	○	○
Jade: 8 in X 5 in X 5 in Seth: 4 in X 11 in X 3 in	○	○
Jade: 3 in X 9 in X 6 in Seth: 8 in X 13 in X 1 in	○	○
Jade: 6 in X 13 in X 4 in Seth: 3 in X 8 in X 2 in	○	○

7. A three-section warehouse holds a total of 24,766 ft³ of volume. The first section has a storage area of 436 ft² and a height of 19 ft. The second section has a height of 15 ft. and a depth of 26 ft. The volume of the first two sections is 17,254 ft³. Based on this information, complete the table below.

Volume of first section in cubic feet	
Length of the second section in feet	
Volume of the third section in cubic feet	

End of Measurement and Data

Chapter 6: Geometry

Lesson 1: Coordinate Geometry

You can scan the QR code given below or use the url to access additional EdSearch resources including videos and mobile apps related to *Coordinate Geometry*.

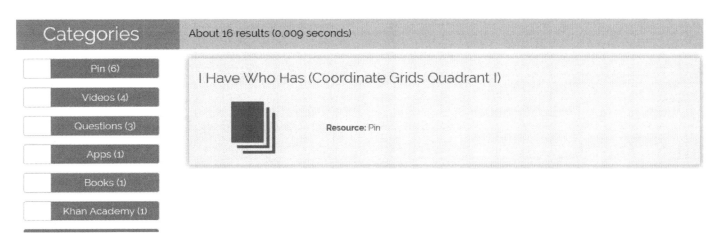

Categories	About 16 results (0.009 seconds)
Pin (6)	**I Have Who Has (Coordinate Grids Quadrant I)**
Videos (4)	
Questions (3)	**Resource:** Pin
Apps (1)	
Books (1)	
Khan Academy (1)	

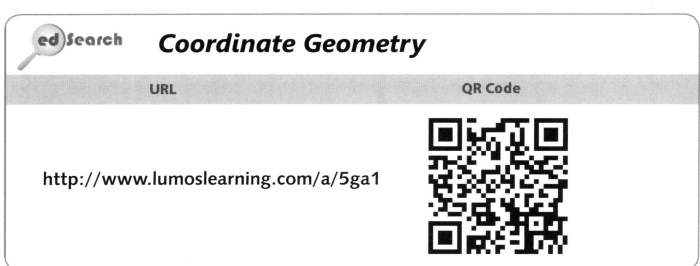

ed)Search   *Coordinate Geometry*

URL	QR Code
http://www.lumoslearning.com/a/5ga1	

1. Assume Point D was added to the grid so that Shape ABCD was a rectangle. Which of these could be the ordered pair for Point D?

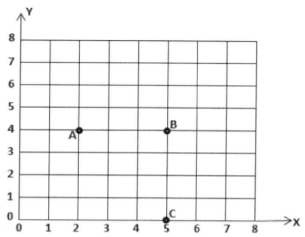

Ⓐ (0, 0)
Ⓑ (0, 2)
Ⓒ (2, 0)
Ⓓ (2, 2)

2. Assume Segments AB and BC were drawn. Compare the lengths of the two segments.

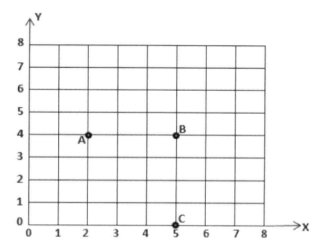

Ⓐ Segment AB is longer than Segment BC.
Ⓑ Segment BC is longer than Segment AB.
Ⓒ Segments AB and BC have the same length.
Ⓓ It cannot be determined from this information.

3.

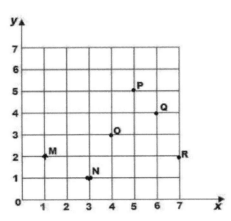

Where is Point R located?

Ⓐ (2, 7)
Ⓑ (7, 2)
Ⓒ (6, 4)
Ⓓ (4, 6)

4. Which point is located at (4, 3)?

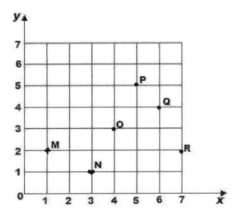

Ⓐ Point N
Ⓑ Point P
Ⓒ Point Q
Ⓓ Point O

5. Locate Point P on the coordinate grid. Which of the following ordered pairs represents its position?

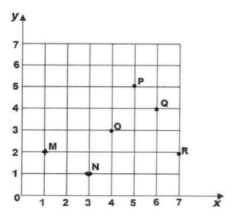

Ⓐ (5, 5)
Ⓑ (3, 1)
Ⓒ (1, 2)
Ⓓ (7, 2)

6. The graph below represents the values listed in the accompanying table, and their linear relationship. Use the graph and the table to respond to the following:
    What is the value of c (in the table)?

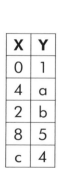

X	Y
0	1
4	a
2	b
8	5
c	4

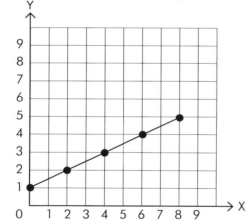

Ⓐ c = 9
Ⓑ c = 7
Ⓒ c = 6
Ⓓ c = 5

7. The graph below represents the values listed in the accompanying table, and their linear relationship. Use the graph and the table to respond to the following:
What is the value of b (in the table)?

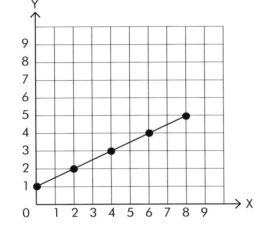

X	Y
0	1
4	a
2	b
8	5
c	4

Ⓐ b = 1
Ⓑ b = 2
Ⓒ b = 3
Ⓓ b = 6

8. Which of the following graphs best represents the values in this table?

x	y
1	1
2	2
3	3

Ⓐ

Ⓑ

Ⓒ

Ⓓ

9. On a coordinate grid, which of these points would be closest to the origin?

    Ⓐ (2, 1)
    Ⓑ (2, 7)
    Ⓒ (1, 5)
    Ⓓ (0, 4)

10. If these four ordered pairs were plotted to form a diamond, which point would be the top of the diamond?

    Ⓐ (2, 4)
    Ⓑ (5, 8)
    Ⓒ (8, 4)
    Ⓓ (5, 0)

11. Points A (3, 2), B (6, 2), C (6, 6) and D (3, 7) are plotted on a coordinate grid. What type of polygon is ABCD?

    Ⓐ a rectangle
    Ⓑ a rhombus
    Ⓒ a parallelogram
    Ⓓ a trapezoid

12. The graph below represents the values listed in the accompanying table, and their linear relationship. Use the graph and the table to respond to the following:
    Which of the following rules describes the behavior of this function?

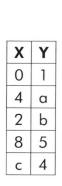

X	Y
0	1
4	a
2	b
8	5
c	4

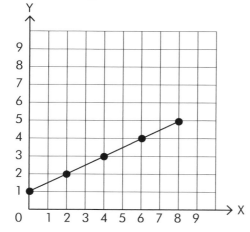

    Ⓐ y is equal to one more than x
    Ⓑ y is equal to twice x
    Ⓒ y is equal to one more than half of x
    Ⓓ y is equal to one more than twice x

13.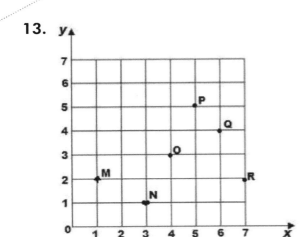

Assume points O, P, and Q form three vertices of a parallelogram. Which ordered pair could be the fourth vertex of that parallelogram?

Ⓐ (3, 3)
Ⓑ (4, 4)
Ⓒ (3, 5)
Ⓓ (3, 4)

14. Which of the following graphs best represents the values in this table?

x	y
3	1
3	2
3	3

Ⓐ
Ⓑ
Ⓒ
Ⓓ

15. **If the functions x = y + 1 and y = 3 were plotted on a coordinate grid, which of these would be true?**

    &Ⓐ They would intersect once.
    Ⓑ They would form parallel lines.
    Ⓒ They would intersect more than once.
    Ⓓ They would form perpendicular lines.

16. **Circle the letter that represents the x- axis.**

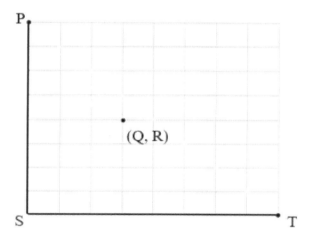

    Ⓐ P
    Ⓑ S
    Ⓒ T

17. Which of the following are the coordinates of points A, B and C? Circle the correct answer choice.

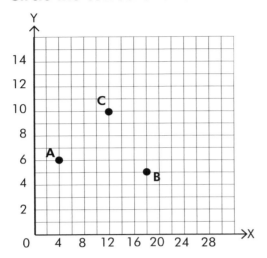

Ⓐ Point A: (2,6); Point B: (9,5); Point C: (6, 10)

Ⓑ Point A: (4,6); Point B: (12, 10); Point C: (18,5)

Ⓒ Point A: (4,6); Point B: (18, 5); Point C: (12,10)

Ⓓ Point A: (6,4); Point B: (10,12); Point C: (18,5)

Chapter 6

Lesson 2: Real World Graphing Problems

You can scan the QR code given below or use the url to access additional EdSearch resources including videos and mobile apps related to *Real World Graphing Problems*.

 **Real World Graphing Problems**

URL	QR Code
http://www.lumoslearning.com/a/5ga2	

1. According to the map, what is the location of the weather station (⚡)?

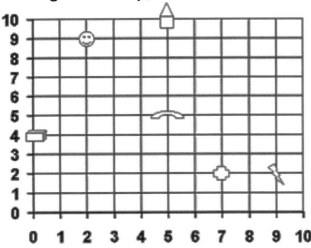

Ⓐ (3,9)
Ⓑ (8,2)
Ⓒ (9,2)
Ⓓ (2,9)

2. According to the map, what is the location of the warehouse (▱)?

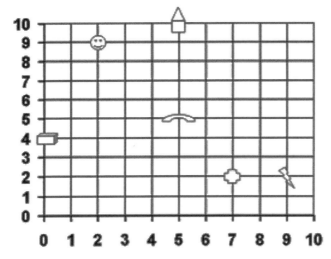

Ⓐ (x = 4)
Ⓑ (0,4)
Ⓒ (y = 4)
Ⓓ (4,0)

3. According to the map, which is located at (7,2)?

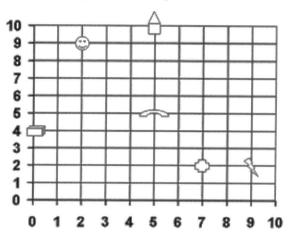

Ⓐ The hospital

Ⓑ The bridge

Ⓒ The playground

Ⓓ The house

4. According to the map, which is located at (5,5)?

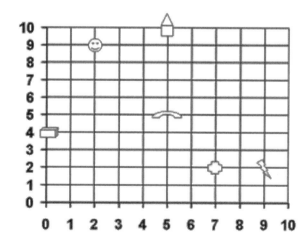

Ⓐ The hospital

Ⓑ The bridge

Ⓒ The playground

Ⓓ The house

5. Which set of directions would lead a person from the playground (☺) to the hospital (✚)?

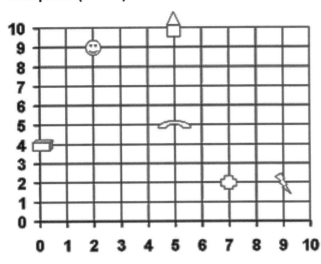

Ⓐ Walk 5 units along -ve y-axis and 7 units along +ve x-axis.
Ⓑ Walk 7 units along -ve y-axis and 2 units along +ve x-axis.
Ⓒ Walk 2 units along -ve y-axis and 7 units along +ve x-axis.
Ⓓ Walk 7 units along -ve y-axis and 5 units along +ve x-axis.

6. Which set of directions would lead a person from the weather station (⚡) to the bridge (⌒)?

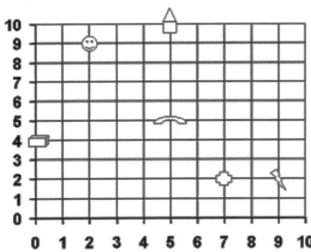

Ⓐ Walk 5 units along -ve x-axis and 5 units along +ve y-axis.
Ⓑ Walk 2 units along -ve x-axis and 0 units along +ve y-axis.
Ⓒ Walk 4 units along -ve x-axis and 3 units along +ve y-axis.
Ⓓ Walk 3 units along -ve x-axis and 4 units along +ve y-axis.

7. Where should the town locate a new lumber mill so it is as close as possible to both the warehouse (△) and the hospital (✛)?

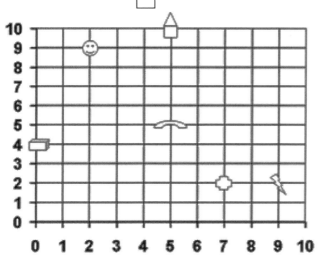

Ⓐ (7,0)
Ⓑ (5,3)
Ⓒ (1,7)
Ⓓ (5,0)

8. According to the map, what is the location of the zebras (🦓)?

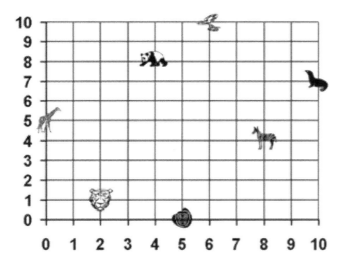

Ⓐ (8,4)
Ⓑ (8,0)
Ⓒ (4,8)
Ⓓ (4,4)

9. According to the map, what is the location of the giraffes ( )?

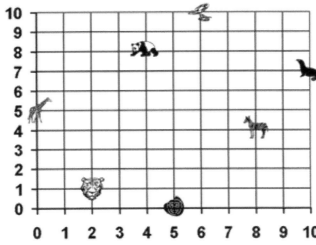

Ⓐ (y = 5)
Ⓑ (0,5)
Ⓒ (x = 5)
Ⓓ (5,0)

10. According to the map, which is located at (10,7)?

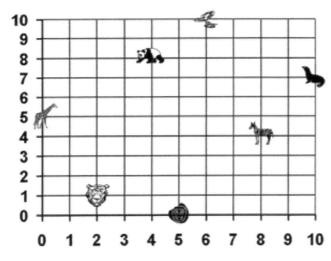

Ⓐ The tigers

Ⓑ The pandas

Ⓒ The snakes

Ⓓ The seals

11. According to the map, which is located at (6,10)?

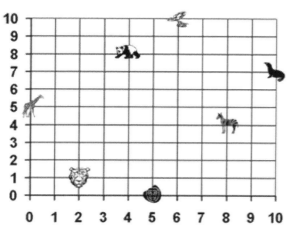

Ⓐ The seals

Ⓑ The monkeys

Ⓒ The snakes

Ⓓ The zebras

12. According to the map, what is the distance (along the grid) from the pandas ( ) to the monkeys ( )?

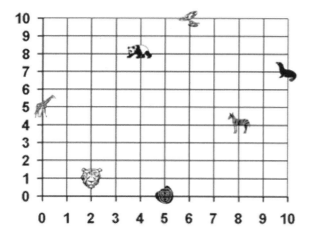

Ⓐ 9 units
Ⓑ 8 units
Ⓒ 1 unit
Ⓓ 6 units

13. Which set of directions would lead a person from the giraffes ( ) to the tigers ( )?

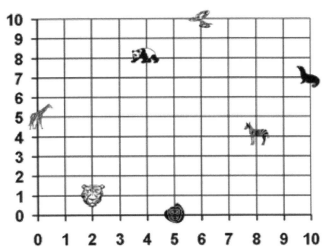

Ⓐ Walk 4 units along the x-axis and 2 units along the y-axis.
Ⓑ Walk 1 unit along the x-axis and 2 units along the y-axis.
Ⓒ Walk 2 units along the x-axis and 4 units along the y-axis.
Ⓓ Walk 4 units along the x-axis and 1 unit along the y-axis.

14. Which would be the best location for the antelopes, so they are as far as possible from the tigers (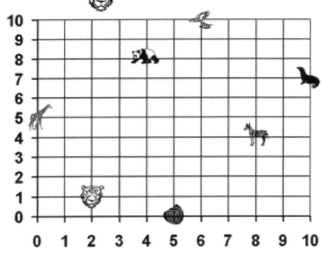)?

Ⓐ (3,3)
Ⓑ (0,4)
Ⓒ (6,1)
Ⓓ (8,8)

15. The graph below shows the total purchase price of game tickets depending on the amount of tickets purchased.

Based on this graph, what is the total cost for twelve tickets? Circle the correct answer choice.

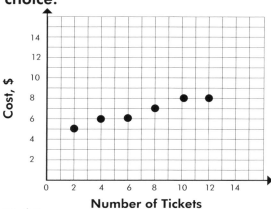

Ⓐ $5
Ⓑ $6
Ⓒ $7
Ⓓ $8

16. During her run, Liu records the number of minutes it took to reach six mile markers. Based on this graph determine if the statements below are true or false.

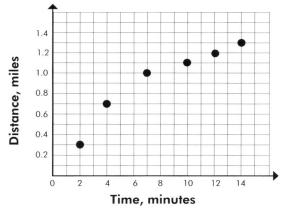

	True	False
Lui reaches mile marker 1.0 in seven minutes.	○	○
It took Lui two minutes to run from mile marker 1.0 to mile marker 1.2.	○	○
Lui ran from mile marker 1.1 to mail marker 1.2 in three minutes.	○	○
Fourteen minutes after Lui started she reached mile marker 1.3.	○	○

17. The weather station is at the coordinates (9,2).
    Plot the coordinate on the graph.

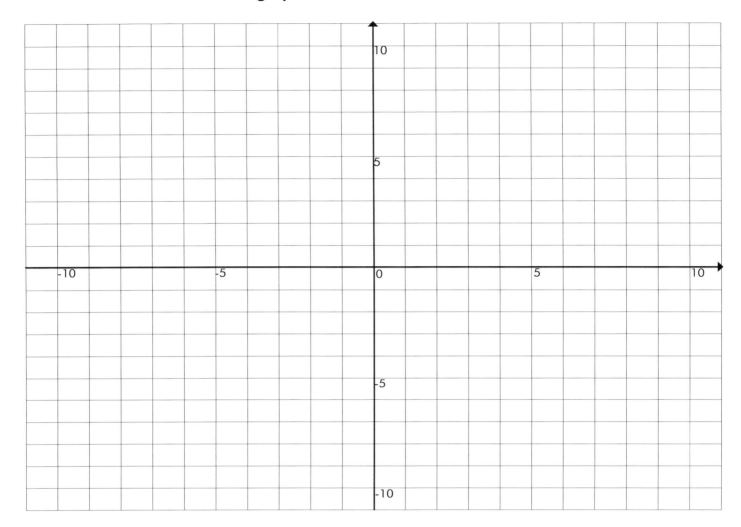

LumosLearning.com

Chapter 6

Lesson 3: Properties of 2D Shapes

You can scan the QR code given below or use the url to access additional EdSearch resources including videos and mobile apps related to *Properties of 2D Shapes*.

 **Properties of 2D Shapes**

URL	QR Code
http://www.lumoslearning.com/a/5gb3	

1. **Complete the following.**
   A plane figure is regular only if it has _____.

   Ⓐ equal sides
   Ⓑ congruent angles
   Ⓒ equal sides and congruent angles
   Ⓓ equal sides, congruent angles, and interior angles that total 180

2. **Complete the following.**
   Two _____ will always be similar.

   Ⓐ circles
   Ⓑ squares
   Ⓒ equilateral triangles
   Ⓓ all of the above

3. **Two interior angles of a triangle measure 30 degrees and 50 degrees. Which type of triangle could it be?**

   Ⓐ a right triangle
   Ⓑ an acute triangle
   Ⓒ an obtuse triangle
   Ⓓ an isosceles triangle

4. **Complete the following.**
   An angle measuring between 0 and 90 degrees is called a(n) _____.

   Ⓐ acute angle
   Ⓑ obtuse angle
   Ⓒ straight angle
   Ⓓ reflex angle

5. **Which of these is not a characteristic of a polygon?**

   Ⓐ a closed shape
   Ⓑ parallel faces
   Ⓒ made of straight lines
   Ⓓ two-dimensional

6. **Complete the following.**
    This isosceles triangle has _____.

    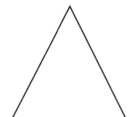

    (A) one line of symmetry
    (B) two congruent angles
    (C) two equal sides
    (D) all of the above

7. Marcus used tape and drinking straws to build the outline of a two-dimensional shape. He used four straws in all. Exactly three of the straws were of equal length. What might Marcus have built?

    (A) a square
    (B) a trapezoid
    (C) a rectangle
    (D) a rhombus

8. How many pairs of parallel sides does a regular octagon have?

    (A) 8
    (B) 4
    (C) 2
    (D) 0

9. A rectangle can be described by all of the following terms except _____.

    (A) a parallelogram
    (B) a polygon
    (C) a prism
    (D) a quadrilateral

10. Which of the following statements is not true?

    (A) An equilateral triangle must have exactly 3 lines of symmetry.
    (B) An equilateral triangle will have at least one 60-degree angle.
    (C) An equilateral triangle must have rotational symmetry.
    (D) All equilateral triangles are congruent.

11. **Which of the following shapes is not a polygon?**

   Ⓐ semicircle
   Ⓑ trapezoid
   Ⓒ hexagon
   Ⓓ decagon

12. **What is the name for a polygon that has an acute exterior angle?**

   Ⓐ convex
   Ⓑ concave
   Ⓒ complex
   Ⓓ simple

13. **How many diagonals does a rectangle have?**

   Ⓐ 1
   Ⓑ 2
   Ⓒ 3
   Ⓓ 4

14. **Which shape is a polygon, a quadrilateral, and a rhombus?**

   Ⓐ an isosceles triangle
   Ⓑ a rectangle
   Ⓒ a square
   Ⓓ a trapezoid

15. **Which of the following terms does not describe a trapezoid?**

   Ⓐ a parallelogram
   Ⓑ a polygon
   Ⓒ a quadrilateral
   Ⓓ a quadrangle

Name ______________________ Date ______________

16. **Read the statements below and indicate whether they are true or false.**

	True	False
All squares are rhombuses.	◯	◯
All parallelograms have four right angles.	◯	◯
All trapezoids have at least one set of parallel sides.	◯	◯
All squares are rectangles.	◯	◯

17. **Circle the word below that describes all trapezoids.**

Ⓐ Parallelogram

Ⓑ Rhombus

Ⓒ Square

Ⓓ Quadrilateral

Chapter 6

Lesson 4: Classifying 2D Shapes

You can scan the QR code given below or use the url to access additional EdSearch resources including videos and mobile apps related to *Classifying 2D Shapes*.

 **Classifying 2D Shapes**

URL	QR Code
http://www.lumoslearning.com/a/5gb4	

1. **Which shape belongs in the center of the diagram?**

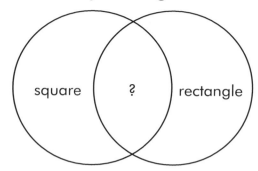

square   ?   rectangle

Ⓐ triangle
Ⓑ circle
Ⓒ square
Ⓓ polygon

2. **Which shape belongs in section B of the diagram?**

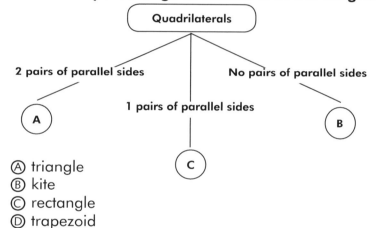

Quadrilaterals

2 pairs of parallel sides   No pairs of parallel sides

1 pairs of parallel sides

A   C   B

Ⓐ triangle
Ⓑ kite
Ⓒ rectangle
Ⓓ trapezoid

3. **Which shape belongs in section C of the diagram?**

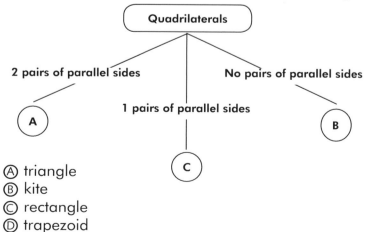

Quadrilaterals

2 pairs of parallel sides   No pairs of parallel sides

1 pairs of parallel sides

A   C   B

Ⓐ triangle
Ⓑ kite
Ⓒ rectangle
Ⓓ trapezoid

4. **Which shape does not belong in section A of the diagram?**

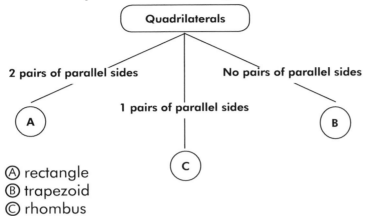

Ⓐ rectangle
Ⓑ trapezoid
Ⓒ rhombus
Ⓓ square

5. **Which shape belongs in section A of the diagram?**

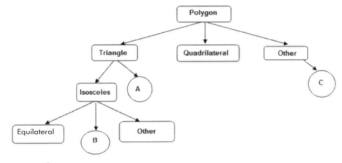

Ⓐ scalene
Ⓑ right
Ⓒ acute
Ⓓ symmetrical

6. **Which shape belongs in section B of the diagram?**

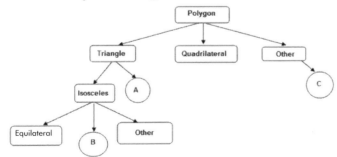

Ⓐ Scalene
Ⓑ Isosceles Right
Ⓒ Acute
Ⓓ Symmetrical

7. **Which shape does not belong in section C of the diagram?**

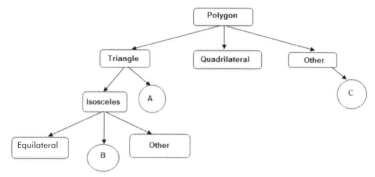

Ⓐ Octagon
Ⓑ Decagon
Ⓒ Pentagon
Ⓓ Rhombus

8. **Which statement is true?**

Ⓐ All triangles are quadrangles.
Ⓑ All polygons are hexagons.
Ⓒ All parallelograms are polygons.
Ⓓ All parallelograms are rectangles.

9. **Which statement is false?**

Ⓐ All octagons are parallelograms.
Ⓑ All rectangles are quadrangles.
Ⓒ All triangles are polygons.
Ⓓ All rectangles are quadrilaterals.

10. **Which statement defines a quadrangle?**

Ⓐ Any rectangle that has 4 sides of equal length
Ⓑ Any quadrilateral with 2 pairs of parallel sides
Ⓒ Any polygon with 4 angles
Ⓓ Any polygon with 4 or more sides

11. Which shape is a quadrilateral but not a parallelogram?

Ⓐ

Ⓑ

Ⓒ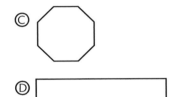

Ⓓ

12. Which shape is a rhombus but not a square?

Ⓐ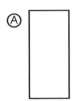

Ⓑ

Ⓒ

Ⓓ

13. In a hierarchy of shapes, how could the category of "pentagon" be split in two?

Ⓐ polygon and non-polygon
Ⓑ 5 sides and 6 sides
Ⓒ parallelogram and not parallelogram
Ⓓ regular and non-regular

LumosLearning.com

14. Which triangle would be classified as equiangular?

Ⓐ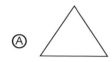

Ⓑ

Ⓒ

Ⓓ

15. Which shape would not be classified as regular?

Ⓐ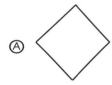

Ⓑ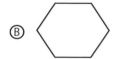

Ⓒ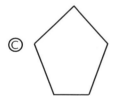

Ⓓ

16. Circle the shape that is a parallelogram with four equal sides and one of the angles measuring 55 degrees

Ⓐ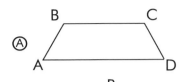

Ⓑ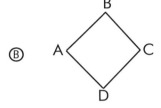

Ⓒ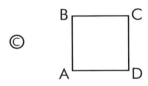

Ⓓ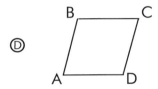

17. Which of the following quadrilaterals has all the properties listed below?

· At least one pair of parallel sides.
· Opposites sides are equal.
· All sides are congruent.
· Not all angles are equal.

Ⓐ Rhombus
Ⓑ Trapezoid
Ⓒ Rectangle
Ⓓ Square

End of Geometry

GMAS FAQs

What will GMAS Assessment Look Like?

In many ways, the GMAS assessments will be unlike anything many students have ever seen. The tests will be conducted online, requiring students complete tasks to assess a deeper understanding of the Georgia standards. The students will take the Summative Assessment at the end of the year.

The time for the Math Summative assessment for each grade is given below:

Estimated Time on Task in Minutes		
Grade	Section 1	Section 2
3	65	65
4	65	65
5	65	65
6	65	65
7	65	65
8	65	65

How is this Lumos tedBook aligned to GMAS Guidelines?

The practice tests provided in the Lumos Program were created to reflect the depth and rigor of the GMAS assessments based on the information published by the test administrator. However, the content and format of the GMAS assessment that is officially administered to the students could be different compared to these practice tests. You can get more information about this test by visiting https://www.gadoe.org/Curriculum-Instruction-and-Assessment/Assessment/Pages/EOG-Study-Resource-Guides.aspx

What item types are included in the Online GMAS Test?

Because the assessment is online, the test will consist of a combination of new types of questions:

1. Selected Response or Multiple choice questions
2. Multi select or two part questions
3. Drag and Drop
4. Hot text
5. Equation editor
6. Plot the point
7. Bar chart

For more information on 2021-22 Assessment year, visit

http://www.lumoslearning.com/a/gmas-2021-faqs

OR Scan the **QR Code**

Discover Engaging and Relevant Learning Resources

Lumos EdSearch is a safe search engine specifically designed for teachers and students. Using EdSearch, you can easily find thousands of standards-aligned learning resources such as questions, videos, lessons, worksheets and apps. Teachers can use EdSearch to create custom resource kits to perfectly match their lesson objective and assign them to one or more students in their classroom.

To access the EdSearch tool, use the search box after you log into Lumos StepUp or use the link provided below.

http://www.lumoslearning.com/a/edsearchb	

The Lumos Standards Coherence map provides information about previous level, next level and related standards. It helps educators and students visually explore learning standards. It's an effective tool to help students progress through the learning objectives. Teachers can use this tool to develop their own pacing charts and lesson plans. Educators can also use the coherence map to get deep insights into why a student is struggling in a specific learning objective.

Teachers can access the Coherence maps after logging into the StepUp Teacher Portal or use the link provided below.

http://www.lumoslearning.com/a/coherence-map	

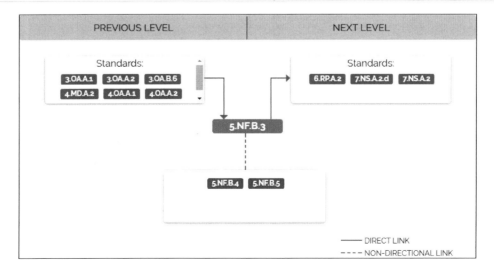

What if I buy more than one Lumos Study Program?

Step 1

Visit the URL and login to your account.
http://www.lumoslearning.com

Step 2

Click on 'My tedBooks' under the "Account" tab.
Place the Book Access Code and submit.

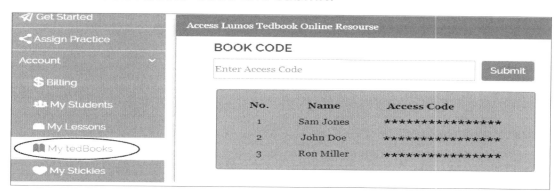

Step 3

To add the new book for a registered student, choose the
⊙ Existing Student button and select the student and submit.

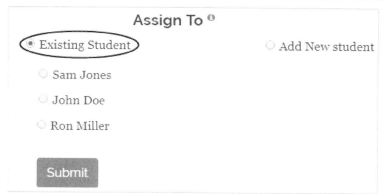

To add the new book for a new student, choose the ⊙ Add New student
button and complete the student registration.

Assign To ⓞ

   ○ Existing Student   ⊙ Add New student

Register Your TedBook

  Student Name:*   Enter First Name   Enter Last Name

  Student Login*

  Password*

Submit

Lumos StepUp® Mobile App FAQ For Students

What is the Lumos StepUp® App?

It is a FREE application you can download onto your Android Smartphones, tablets, iPhones, and iPads.

What are the Benefits of the StepUp® App?

This mobile application gives convenient access to Practice Tests, Common Core State Standards, Online Workbooks, and learning resources through your Smartphone and tablet computers.

- Fourteen Technology enhanced question types in both MATH and ELA
- Sample questions for Arithmetic drills
- Standard specific sample questions
- Instant access to the Common Core State Standards

Do I Need the StepUp® App to Access Online Workbooks?

No, you can access Lumos StepUp® Online Workbooks through a personal computer. The StepUp® app simply enhances your learning experience and allows you to conveniently access StepUp® Online Workbooks and additional resources through your smartphone or tablet.

How can I Download the App?

Visit **lumoslearning.com/a/stepup-app** using your Smartphone or tablet and follow the instructions to download the app.

QR Code
for Smartphone
Or Tablet Users

Lumos StepUp® Mobile App FAQ For Parents and Teachers

What is the Lumos StepUp® App?

It is a free app that teachers can use to easily access real-time student activity information as well as assign learning resources to students. Parents can also use it to easily access school-related information such as homework assigned by teachers and PTA meetings. It can be downloaded onto smartphones and tablets from popular App Stores.

What are the Benefits of the Lumos StepUp® App?

It provides convenient access to

- Standards aligned learning resources for your students
- An easy to use Dashboard
- Student progress reports
- Active and inactive students in your classroom
- Professional development information
- Educational Blogs

How can I Download the App?

Visit **lumoslearning.com/a/stepup-app** using your Smartphone or tablet and follow the instructions to download the app.

QR Code
for Smartphone
Or Tablet Users

Progress Chart

Standard		Lesson	Page No.	Practice		Mastered	Re-practice /Reteach
GMAS	CCSS			Date	Score		
MGSE5.OA.1	5.OA.A.1	Write & Interpret Numerical Expressions & Patterns	10				
MGSE5.OA.2	5.OA.A.2	Record and Interpret Calculations with Numbers	13				
MGSE5.OA.3	5.OA.B.3	Analyze Patterns and Relationships	16				
MGSE5.NBT.1	5.NBT.A.1	Place Value	25				
MGSE5.NBT.2	5.NBT.A.2	Multiplication & Division of Powers of Ten	29				
MGSE5.NBT.3	5.NBT.A.3.	Read and Write Decimals	33				
MGSE5.NBT.3	5.NBT.A.3.	Comparing and Ordering Decimals	37				
MGSE5.NBT.4	5.NBT.A.4	Rounding Decimals	41				
MGSE5.NBT.5	5.NBT.B.5	Multiplication of Whole Numbers	45				
MGSE5.NBT.6	5.NBT.B.6	Division of Whole Numbers	49				
MGSE5.NBT.7	5.NBT.B.7	Add, Subtract, Multiply, and Divide Decimals	53				
MGSE5.NF.1	5.NF.A.1	Add & Subtract Fractions	57				
MGSE5.NF.2	5.NF.A.2	Problem Solving with Fractions	63				
MGSE5.NF.3	5.NF.B.3	Interpreting Fractions	68				
MGSE5.NF.4	5.NF.B.4	Multiply Fractions	72				
MGSE5.NF.4b	5.NF.B.4.B	Multiply to Find Area	77				

Standard		Lesson	Page No.	Practice		Mastered	Re-practice /Reteach
GMAS	CCSS			Date	Score		
MGSE5.NF.5a	5.NF.B.5.A	Multiplication as Scaling	82				
MGSE5.NF.5b	5.NF.B.5.B	Numbers Multiplied by Fractions	86				
MGSE5.NF.6	5.NF.B.6	Real World Problems with Fractions	90				
MGSE5.NF.7a	5.NF.B.7.A	Dividing Fractions	95				
MGSE5.NF.7b	5.NF.B.7.B	Dividing by Unit Fractions	99				
MGSE5.NF.7c	5.NF.B.7.C	Real World Problems Dividing Fractions	103				
MGSE5.MD.1	5.MD.A.1	Converting Units of Measure	107				
N/A	5.MD.B.2	Representing and Interpreting Data	111				
N/A	5.MD.C.3.A	Volume	127				
N/A	5.MD.C.3.B	Cubic Units	132				
N/A	5.MD.C.4	Counting Cubic Units	136				
MGSE5.MD.5a	5.MD.C.5.A	Multiply to Find Volume	141				
MGSE5.MD.5b	5.MD.C.5.B	Real World Problems with Volume	145				
MGSE5.MD.5c	5.MD.C.5.C	Adding Volumes	149				
MGSE5.G.1	5.G.A.1	Coordinate Geometry	152				
MGSE5.G.2	5.G.A.2	Real World Graphing Problems	161				
MGSE5.G.3	5.G.B.3	Properties of 2D Shapes	171				
MGSE5.G.4	5.G.B.4	Classifying 2D Shapes	176				

Lumos Learning
Developed by Expert Teachers

Grade 5

GEORGIA
ENGLISH
LANGUAGE ARTS LITERACY
GMAS Practice

Student Copy

Updated for 2021-22

(((tedBook)))
ONLINE

2 GMAS Practice Tests
7 Question Types

Available
- At Leading book stores
- Online www.LumosLearning.com

Made in the USA
Middletown, DE
11 March 2022

62364597R00108